THE ALCHEMIST

Ben Jonson

Edited by Peter Bement

ROUTLEDGE

LONDON AND NEW YORK

First published in 1987 by
Methuen & Co. Ltd

Reprinted 1990, 1992 by
Routledge
11 New Fetter Lane
London EC4P 4EE
29 West 35th Street
New York NY 10001

Introduction, Critical commentary
and Notes © 1987 Peter Bement

Printed in England by
Clays Ltd, St Ives plc

British Library Cataloguing in
Publication Data

Jonson, Ben
    The alchemist. – (Routledge English
    texts).
    I. Title II. Bement, Peter
    822'.3   PR2605

    ISBN 0 415 05135 5

Library of Congress Cataloguing in
Publication Data

Jonson, Ben 1573?–1637.
    The alchemist.
    (Routledge English texts)
    Bibliography: p.
    I. Bement, Peter. II. Title. III. Series.
PR2605.A2B464   1987   822'.3
87–10984

    ISBN 0 415 05135 5

For my Father and Mother

Contents

Acknowledgements

My debt to previous editors, scholars and critics of *The Alchemist* is too large to record in detail, but special mention must be made of the indispensable edition by Herford and Simpson (Oxford, 1937), and that of F. H. Mares (The Revels Plays, London, 1967). My thanks are due to Professor Gwynne Edwards for help with Surly's Spanish. I am grateful for valuable assistance from the staffs of the National Library of Wales, the University College of Wales Library, and the data preparation room of the college's Computer Unit.

Peter Bement
Aberystwyth, 1986

Introduction

Ben Jonson was born, probably in London, in 1572 or 1573, a month after the death of his father, a minister of religion. His mother later married a master bricklayer, and Jonson was always to resent the circumstances of his early years: he told William Drummond that he had been 'brought up poorly'. His education at Westminster School, where he studied under William Camden, was interrupted when, very much against his inclination, he was apprenticed to his stepfather as a bricklayer. During the period of his apprenticeship he got married, and served as a soldier in Flanders. By 1597, however, he had joined a company of strolling players, and shortly afterwards begins to appear in the accounts of Philip Henslowe, owner of the Rose Theatre, as a writer working for his company, the Admiral's Men. But his first really successful play, *Every Man in his Humour*, was acted in 1598 by the Lord Chamberlain's Men, later to be the King's Men, of which Shakespeare was a member. There followed three plays, called by Jonson 'comical satires': *Every Man out of his Humour* (1599), *Cynthia's Revels* (1600) and *Poetaster* (1601). These plays, very different from one another, are all experiments in giving to comedy the harsh, biting manner of verse satire, and also, incidentally, form part of that exchange of insults with his fellow dramatists John Marston and Thomas Dekker that became known as the 'War of the Theatres'. His two tragedies, *Sejanus* (1603) and *Catiline* (1611), remarkable though they are, were in varying degrees failures on the stage, and Jonson's enduring fame as a playwright rests on four great comedies: *Volpone* (1605/6), for the King's Men; *Epicoene* (1609), for the Children of Her Majesty's Revels; *The Alchemist* (1610), again for the King's Men; and *Bartholomew Fair* (1614), for the Lady Elizabeth's Men.

Jonson's achievements were not confined to the playhouse; indeed, he was never, like Shakespeare, a full-time resident playwright with one particular company, and worked only sporadically in the theatre. From 1602 he was able to rely on the patronage of Sir Robert Townshend and later Esmé Stuart, Lord Aubigny; and in 1605 he began writing masques to celebrate festive occasions at court. In collaboration with the designer Inigo Jones and the leading musicians and choreographers of the day, Jonson shaped the development of these spectacular performances, writing the dialogue and the elegant songs and lyrics, and devising the symbolic action that provided the framework for the dancing of the courtly participants and the magical effects of Jones's ingenious perspective scenes. Jonson himself considered his most important work to be his non-dramatic poetry: his 'Epigrams' he described as 'the ripest of my studies', and his handling of such forms as the verse epistle, the topographical poem and the ode, as well as the polished craftsmanship of his lyric poems, exercised a profound influence upon the course of English poetry during the seventeenth century and thereafter. This influence was cemented by the admiration and friendship of the numerous younger writers, Thomas Carew and Robert Herrick among them, with whom he regularly met in the Apollo room of the Devil Tavern, and who became known as the 'sons of Ben'. In *Timber, or Discoveries*, published posthumously in 1640, Jonson left behind him an informal series of essays and observations upon life and literature that gives valuable insight into his literary practice. The great Folio edition of his *Works* that Jonson published in 1616 also bears witness to the seriousness with which he regarded his profession as a writer, and contained all of his writings up to 1612 (including plays, to the surprise and derision of some of his contemporaries who could not see how plays could be regarded as 'works') that he wished to preserve. The Folio established Jonson as the leading literary figure of his day, and led to the granting of a royal pension in the same year, confirming him as England's unofficial Laureate.

There followed nine confident years in which he wrote only masques and non-dramatic verse, but troubles also began to beset him. In 1623 a fire destroyed his library together with manuscripts of works in progress (commemorated in his poem, 'An Execration upon Vulcan'). With the accession of Charles I in 1625, he began to lose favour at court, and his quarrel with Inigo Jones over whether the poet or the painter should be in control soured his career as maker of court masques. Even the sinecure of Official Chronologer to the City of London, in which he succeeded Thomas Middleton in 1627, ran into difficulties, and the stipend was not paid between 1631 and 1634. Financial troubles forced him back to the public theatres, but his new comedies, though in their way original and inventive, never recaptured his earlier success: the failure of *The New Inn* (1629) was a particularly bitter blow. His health failed too: in 1628 he was partially paralysed by a stroke, and seems to have been confined to his room until his death in 1637.

Jonson's theatrical and literary achievements are informed by his high conception of poetry as the instrument of civilization. The poet, he argues in *Discoveries*,

> can feign a commonwealth ... [and] can govern it with councils, strengthen it with laws, correct it with judgements, inform it with religion and morals. ... We do not require in him mere elocution or an excellent faculty in verse, but the exact knowledge of all virtues and their contraries; with ability to render the one loved, the other hated, by his proper embattling them.

This social function of literature means that Jonson's is often an art of encomium, and he wrote many poems in praise of the personages, sometimes scholarly, more frequently aristocratic, that he thought embodied most fully the public and private virtues he admired. His court masques hold up before king and court a Platonic mirror in which they see ideal images of themselves. What may look like flattery to a modern eye is really a discreet didacticism, reminding those with great social and political power of their equally great responsibilities. The obverse of encomium is satire, and much of Jonson's most vigorous writing, dramatic and non-dramatic, depicts the shortcomings of a world that could never, in truth, live up to his expectations. Satire, indeed, is the natural weapon of a conservative idealist such as Jonson, allowing him to acknowledge life's grotesque imperfections while ostensibly seeking to reform them.

Jonson's interpretation of poetry's social function also made the poet a public man. Jonson himself becomes a dramatic presence in his poetry, the erudite, principled, sometimes aggressive champion of humane values; often cantankerous, but also inviting a comical awareness of his physique, his 'mountain belly' and his 'rocky face' ('My Picture Left in Scotland'). The reader of The Alchemist encounters this literary personality in the prefatory material to the play. In the dedicatory epistle Jonson celebrates with a characteristic tone of reverent familiarity the aristocratic virtues of his friend Lady Wroth. In the preface 'To the Reader' he demands the understanding that he always sought for his non-theatrical writings, as when, in the first of his 'Epigrams', he addresses the reader thus:

> Pray thee take care, that tak'st my book in hand,
> To read it well: that is, to understand.

Such understanding, he sometimes felt, could only be expected from scholarly friends such as John Selden. This is the Jonson of austere scholarly and aesthetic standards, who boasted to William Drummond that he 'knew more in Greek and Latin than all the poets in England', despite his incomplete formal education, and who, in his discussions of verse writing in Discoveries, emphasizes 'art', by which he means painstaking craftsmanship and imitation of the best classical models, though 'nature' (native genius) is also given its due place. The attack, in the preface to *The Alchemist*, upon the corrupt standards of the contemporary theatre is very much of a piece with this, but there are also hints here of his uneasy relationship with the theatre, always ready to flare up into a massive disdain when one of his plays was badly received or (as he considered) misunderstood:

> And since our dainty age
>   Cannot endure reproof,
> Make not thyself a page,
> To that strumpet the stage,
>   But sing high and aloof,
> Safe from the wolf's black jaw and dull ass's hoof.
>
> ('An Ode to Himself')

Perhaps this same unease underlies the confident lecture to his audience about their responses to the play in the Prologue.

Something of the more informal side of this personality can be glimpsed in the *Conversations with William Drummond*. In 1618 Jonson set out to walk to Scotland, and in the course of his tour visited the poet William Drummond at his estate in Hawthornden. Unaware that his host would record his conversation, Jonson talks scurrilously about the literary figures and great men of the day, tells jokes and anecdotes (some of them off-colour), reminisces, boasts, and clearly enjoys impressing his provincial host, who seems to have been shrewder than he suspected. Drummond concluded:

> He is a great lover and praiser of himself, a contemner of others, given rather to lose a friend than a jest, jealous of every word and action of those about him (especially after drink, which is one of the elements in which he liveth), a dissembler of ill parts which reign in him, a bragger of some good that he wanteth, thinketh nothing well but what either he himself or some of his friends and countrymen hath said or done, he is passionately kind and angry,

careless either to gain or keep, vindictive, but, if he be well answered, at himself.

He told Drummond that he had once 'cozened a lady' by disguising himself as an old astrologer 'in a long gown and a white beard at the light of dim-burning candles'. Whether the story, so strongly reminiscent of the roguery of *The Alchemist*, is true or not is beside the point. It is the fact that Jonson could tell it of himself that is so revealing. He also told Drummond of two killings:

> In his service in the Low Countries, he had, in the face of both the camps, killed an enemy and taken *opima spolia* from him; and since his coming to England, being appealed to the fields, he had killed his adversary, which had hurt him in the arm, and whose sword was ten inches longer than his; for the which he was imprisoned, and almost at the gallows.

The first incident, for which we have only Jonson's word, is made to sound like an episode from a classical epic poem; but the second, the slaying, in 1598, of his fellow actor Gabriel Spencer, suggests a turbulent reality more difficult to square with learned ideals: Jonson only escaped execution by 'benefit of clergy' (being able to read his 'neck verse'), and was released with a brand on his thumb, his goods confiscated. Nor was this his only spell in prison. In the previous year he had spent two months in gaol for his part, as actor and reviser, in Nashe's scurrilous *Isle of Dogs*; and again in 1604 he was imprisoned with his collaborators in *Eastward Ho!*, Chapman and Marston. Only the intervention of powerful friends secured their release and prevented them from having 'their ears and noses cut' as a punishment for the play's anti-Scots satire. There had been trouble, too, over *Sejanus* in 1603, resulting in an appearance before the Privy Council. And in 1606 Jonson and his wife were summoned before the Consistory Court to answer a charge of recusancy (failure to attend services of the established church): Jonson had become a Catholic while in prison in 1598, and only returned to Anglicanism in 1610.

Drummond also reports that Jonson 'hath consumed a whole night in lying looking to his great toe, about which he hath seen Tartars and Turks, Romans and Carthaginians, fight in his imagination', and concludes that he was 'Oppressed with fantasy, which hath overmastered his reason, a general disease in many poets'. We catch sight here of what has usually been regarded as the repressed side to the 'official' Jonson, a side that modern criticism has increasingly wanted to discern in *The Alchemist*. The censorious Jonson, the moralist and aesthetic theorizer of *Discoveries*, seems open to, perhaps even obsessed by, the vitality and disorder of London's teeming low-life, and the sheer eccentricity of its characters. The satiric condemnation of roguery, social chaos, moral licence, fantastic ambition and verbal indulgence may be coloured by fascination, celebration, gleeful disgust, dread. It is in the light of this possibility that Jonson's theoretic statements about comedy should be read.

COMIC THEORY

In the preface he wrote for the revised version of his early play *Every Man in his Humour*, Jonson rejected the frivolity and romantic improbability of Shakespeare's dramatic practice and argued for a realistic and didactic comedy based on neo-classical principles of dramaturgy. In place of the rambling plots and vast time-schemes popular on the contemporary stage, Jonson proposes

> deeds and language such as men do use;
> And persons such as comedy would choose
> When she would show an image of the times,
> And sport with human follies, not with crimes.
> Except we make 'em such by loving still
> Our popular errors, as you'll all confess
> By laughing at them, they deserve no less;
> Which when you heartily do, there's hope left then:
> You that have so graced monsters, may like men.

The 'monsters' of romantic comedy are, it is implied, out of touch with the realistic, humanizing moral concerns of genuine comedy.

The Prologue to *The Alchemist* declares its aim to be the exposure of the 'manners' and 'vices' of the time in order to 'better' its audience. For this moralistic, neo-classical tradition, Sir Philip Sidney (to whose niece the play is dedicated) was the great English spokesman. In his *Apology for Poetry* (1589), he had ridiculed the failure of English romantic drama to accord with neo-classical conceptions of dramatic probability and decorum, and expressed vigorous disapproval of comedy that sought only to provoke laughter by the antics of 'deformed creatures' rather than delight in comic characters designed for didactic purposes. Sidney defines true comedy as 'an imitation of the common errors of our life' represented 'in the most ridiculous and scornful sort that may be, so as it is impossible that any beholder can be content to be such a one'. This definition extends into comic theory the formula (derived from Horace's *Art of Poetry*) that is central to Sidney's defence of literature in general: that it should, and does, 'delight and teach'. The two elements are inextricable in Sidney's theory, literature's pleasurable appeal to the mind enabling the reception of moral truths and precepts for good living. In the case of comedy, the enjoyment of the absurd is allied to the establishment or confirmation of sound ethical judgement in the audience. Jonson faithfully follows Sidney in *Discoveries* by rejecting comedy that aims to 'stir mean affections and provoke for the most part to laughter', and concludes, rather oddly for the writer of so funny a play as *The Alchemist,* that 'the moving of laughter is a fault in comedy, a kind of turpitude, that depraves some part of a man's nature'. The Prologue to *The Alchemist* also reflects the Horatian formula of 'delight and teach' in such phrases as 'fair correctives', and asserts the didactic function of comedy. No doubt we will be led into moral awareness and serious thought, but the stern simplicities of Jonson's critical language should not blind us to the complex energies of the play itself.

THE PLAY AND ITS WORLD

The play's satire on greed and social disintegration can be seen as a response to the economic and political conditions of Jacobean England. A twofold political crisis was looming. The financial needs of the crown, as inflation eroded the yield of crown lands, had increasingly through the sixteenth century to be met by parliament, and under James I the relationship between crown and parliament was beginning to manifest the serious tensions that were to result in the civil war. There was also the religious question. England was an officially Protestant country, the citizens of which were, by law, members of the Church of England. The Elizabethan religious settlement had, nevertheless, compromised on certain key issues of reform in order to accommodate those who might otherwise have been reluctant to accept the new religion, and also to forestall reprisals by the Catholic powers of Europe. The Catholic question, kept alive by such events as the gunpowder plot of 1605, dominated national politics, but there remained a large group, who became known as the Puritans, who demanded more thoroughgoing and consistently Protestant reform of the church. They objected to the retention of what they held to be vestiges of popery in the hierarchy, liturgy and vestments of the church, proposing a preaching ministry and a church organized along New Testament lines. But they lost the political battle, and after the Hampton Court conference (1604) many Puritan clergy were excommunicated. Puritanism became the party of constitutional reform and the focus for the various discontents provoked by the claims of monarchical prerogative, now closely identified with episcopacy. (James had said 'no bishop, no king'.) It is on these political grounds that Jonson became a persistent opponent of Puritanism. In *The Alchemist* he gives anti-Puritan satire a further twist by representing the Protestant cause in its most extreme form. The Anabaptists, unlike the English Puritans, demanded not the reform of the established church but its destruction, and were persecuted throughout northern Europe as a feared revolutionary sect. They proclaimed the kingdom of God on earth at Münster in 1534, but after a year of mayhem the rising was brutally suppressed and they were driven into exile and hiding.

Economically, the long-term development of capitalism continued to shape social change in ways that were threatening to traditional ideas about the organization of society. The growth of towns, especially of London, the decline of rural employment as a result of enclosures, and the rise of a new kind of power based upon money rather than landholdings, tended to undermine institutions of government that expressed medieval notions of a social hierarchy functioning by personal loyalty and mutual obligation. The problems associated with the growing power of money were exacerbated by periods of rapid inflation throughout the sixteenth century, caused partly by influxes of precious metals from the new world which cheapened many European currencies, but also by more complex mechanisms of the domestic economy itself, such as the pressures of an increasing population against a vulnerable food supply, and inappropriate fiscal policies. Technical understanding of these phenomena was almost nonexistent, and the conventional response was to analyse them according to moral criteria, ascribing economic ills to the decline among the nobility of 'hospitality' and proper responsibility for their lands and tenants, to the corruption and selfishness of public officials and the greed of merchants.

Jonson adopts this conservative stance in *The Alchemist*. The various characters of the play are recognizably drawn from a cross-section of Jacobean society and can be seen as representing the decline of the 'common weal' and its 'estates'. Mammon, for example, belongs to the estate of knighthood, its ideals of faith, self-discipline and service undermined by the pursuit of money. His profoundly insincere projection of philanthropic schemes well illustrates the decay of social obligation in an upper class perverted by greed. The church has become Ananias and Tribulation, busily trading off religious principle for cash, and promoting not social stability but political revolution. Dapper proposes to abandon the legal profession for the pursuit of riches at the gaming table, and Drugger will depart from the merchant's normal course of advancement through the livery of his company by marrying into the landed gentry. Kastril, the landed gentleman, is at the same time contemplating the sale of his land to finance a career as a city gallant. The Jonson who, in his poem 'To Penshurst', had idealized a reconstituted aristocratic feudalism can be seen here castigating the corruption and decline of the stable, organic society depicted there.

To this extent, the play might be seen as descending from the invective of Tudor 'complaint' literature against the decay of the traditional social order. More particularly, it is possible to see resemblances to the so-called 'estates plays', a sixteenth-century development into social satire of the morality play's dramatized allegory. There are none the less dangers in seeing the play simply as an array of grotesques that have been assembled by the satirist for judgement. In particular, we misrepresent Jonson's characters if we see their descriptive names and accurate social definition as being the same thing as the abstraction and allegorical reduction of the Virtue and Vice characters of the morality play. And Jonson's 'image of the times' resonates with far more than simple invective in the name of conservative ideals: there is an exhilaration at the energy and the complex vitality of the times that makes itself felt in so remarkable a character as Mammon, who is so very much more than a negative image of abused social privilege and corrupt values. If *The Alchemist*, in many ways a unique play, belongs to any genre, it is to that of 'city comedy', the realistic, satirical comedy of London life that flourished in the early years of the seventeenth century. Jonson himself had played a major part in developing this genre, together with such playwrights as John Marston and Thomas Middleton. Their comedies take a complex, ironic and often ambiguous view of urban life, combining traditional strategies of satire with a sense of excitement at the new men, and the new kinds of power, operating in the amoral world of the city.

PERFORMANCE

The play was first acted in 1610 by the King's Men. Internal evidence (e.g. III.ii.131–2; V.v.102–3) might suggest an intended performance date towards the end of October in that year, but the theatres were closed from mid-July until late November by an outbreak of the plague. Since it would have been extremely unusual for a play to be printed before it was acted, the fact that the play was entered for publication in the Stationers' Register on 3 October 1610, together with evidence of a performance at Oxford in September, could argue for a London opening of the play earlier than 12 July 1610. By 1610 the King's Men were playing not only at the Globe, their large public playhouse on the Bankside, but also at the Blackfriars, a smaller, indoor, 'private' theatre on the other side of the river. That Lovewit's house stands in the Blackfriars district suggests that Jonson had the Blackfriars theatre in mind when writing the play, but external evidence to corroborate this is wanting.

The play was popular, and stayed in the repertory of the King's Men until the theatres were closed by the government in 1642. It was revived at the Restoration, and remained popular in the eighteenth century, especially when Garrick took over the part of Drugger in 1743. After Garrick's retirement in 1776, however, the play continued on the stage only in an abridged version between 1782 and 1787, and, more tenuously, in travesty form as Francis Gentleman's farce, *The Tobacconist*, between 1770 and 1815. In 1899, however, William Poel revived *The Alchemist* for the Elizabethan Stage Society, and the twentieth century has seen a number of performances of the play. Among the most notable productions were the Birmingham Repertory Company's of 1916; that at the Malvern Festival in 1932, with Ralph Richardson as Face and Cedric Hardwicke as Drugger; and the Old Vic's of 1947, with Alec Guinness as a memorable Drugger. More recently, Trevor Nunn's excellent production at the Other Place, Stratford-upon-Avon, in May 1977 (transferred to the Aldwych, London, in December 1977) included Ian McKellen's alarming and sinister reading of Face.

SOURCES

The plot of *The Alchemist*, unusually for a play of this period, is more or less original to its author, but a number of details may be derived from Erasmus's colloquy, *De Alcumista*. Here a crafty priest, pretending to be an alchemical adept, ensnares Balbinus, a man (like Mammon) otherwise intelligent and prudent if it were not for his enthusiasm for alchemy. He parts with considerable sums of money to pay for apparatus, coals, bribes to courtiers and offerings to the Virgin Mary, but all is spent by the priest on whores and gambling. Among the excuses for persistent failure to make gold is a lack of personal holiness in Balbinus (who has neglected his prayers) and the alchemist (guilty of sexual misdemeanours). More important than these resemblances to *The Alchemist*, however, is the suggestion of the rudiments of Jonson's comic method. There is the recognition by the interlocutor in the dialogue that alchemy itself is a metaphor for the way in which the confidence trick 'changes the species of things'. And, when Balbinus is finally tipped off, instead of having the alchemist arrested, he sends him away with yet more money in return for a promise not to expose him to public scorn. The reader is teased with the assertion that 'cheating is a small fault in these sort of cattle' and that Balbinus should not excite our pity because he 'took pleasure in being gulled'. The essence of Erasmus's satire is not invective, but the luring of his readers by means of comedy on to treacherous ground where their unthinking moral responses no longer seem effective. This forces his readers into an admission of complicity in the rogue's dishonest cleverness, and the possibility of having themselves taken pleasure in being gulled by the story. Erasmus thus uses comedy to educate his readers in the difficult task of judgement.

Face's clever improvisations in Act V of *The Alchemist* are loosely based on Plautus' *Mostellaria* (*c.* 200 BC), in which the wily slave Tranio attempts to prevent his master, unexpectedly returned after a long absence, from entering his house and discovering the debaucheries of his son. Tranio's quick wits devise various means of sustaining the illusion that the house is haunted, until at last he is forced to confess, and is forgiven by his master.

Jonson relies on a number of sources for technical and exotic information. These include Martin Delrio's *Disquisitiones Magicae* (1599–1600), which supplies a good deal of the play's alchemical lore and language; and Doll's 'talking fit' regurgitates, half digested, parts of Hugh Broughton's *A Concent of Scripture* (1590).

ALCHEMY

Jonson considered alchemists to be charlatans, as his epigram 'To Alchemists' wittily makes clear:

> If all you boast of your great art be true,
> Sure, willing poverty lives most in you.

Like the modern-day racing tipster and company promoter, the alchemist is peddling a get-rich-quick scheme that has manifestly failed in his own case. In his court masque *Mercury Vindicated from the Alchemists at Court* (1616) Jonson offers a more philosophical objection to alchemy as an art that abuses nature (he thought that arts, and sciences, should *serve* nature), as well as repeating the charges of cozening and cheating. But it is important to realize that few educated men of Jonson's time would have disputed the philosophic basis of alchemical theory, and it is this perhaps that makes alchemy such a potent metaphor in Jonson's comedy of human gullibility.

Alchemy is distinguished by the pursuit of two analogous goals: the means to make gold, and a universal medicine or elixir that would confer health, and even immortality. But, in a wider sense, alchemy was a scientific investigation that sought to understand and to harness the principles of nature for the benefit of man, and under its aegis the beginnings of modern chemistry and pharmacology took shape. In its widest sense, because of its association with religion, the occult and philosophy, it sought to explain man's relation to the cosmos.

The origins of Western alchemy are shrouded in obscurity, but seem to lie in Alexandria and other cities of lower Egypt during the Hellenistic period (approximately 300 BC to AD 300), where the flourishing craft of metallurgy, with its wealth of accumulated practical knowledge about the manipulation of metals, especially precious metals, came into contact with theoretical Greek science and oriental astrology. In the accounts of the alchemists themselves the art began with the mythical figure Hermes Trismegistos, sometimes identified with the Egyptian god Thoth. Some authorities believed that the secrets had been taught by the fallen angels to their human wives, while Arabic sources claimed that God had imparted the alchemical mysteries to Moses and Aaron. Mammon (II.i.80–104) accepts a number of such stories. Alchemical writings down the ages are distinguished by their perverse obscurity and tendency to the cryptic language with which the alchemical adept sought to preserve his mysteries from the uninitiated; and obscurity also provided the stylistic means of conveying his exalted sense of alchemy's dignity and power. Subtle defends the practice (II.iii.198–210).

Alchemy came to Europe in the twelfth century with the translation of Arabic alchemical works into Latin. Four books ascribed to Geber (the Arabic alchemist Jabir ibn-Hayyan), though probably written in Spain during the fourteenth century, were the basic theoretic resource of alchemy for the next 300 years. If the fundamental theories of alchemy were widely accepted during the Renaissance, official attitudes to alchemical gold-making were ambivalent. On the one hand there were attempts by princes and noblemen to control and exploit it, and, on the other, there were attempts to suppress alchemy as a threat to the coinage and the values of precious metals. John Dee was thus licensed by Queen Elizabeth I, and in Prague Maximilian II (1564–76) and Rudolf II (1576–1612) both patronized alchemists. The Englishman Edward Kelly was imprisoned when Rudolf lost patience with his projections, and he died trying to escape. The Elector of Saxony, Christian II, similarly imprisoned – and tortured – the Scot, Alexander Sethon.

By the end of the seventeenth century, alchemy was in decline. Robert Boyle's *The Sceptical Chemist* (1661) attacked the theoretic basis of alchemy; and, although a fitful life continued (in, for example, Sir Isaac Newton's alchemical experiments and the 'phlogiston' theory), by the end of the eighteenth century, when Lavoisier established modern chemistry, alchemy was effectively dead. It has been left to nuclear physics to achieve the transmutation dreamed of by the alchemists.

The transmutation of physical substances was to be achieved through the agency of the 'philosopher's stone', the action of which would be described by a modern chemist as 'catalytic'. In Aristotelian physics, which posited the unity of matter, all physical substances or 'bodies' were thought of as being composed of the same *prima materia* or 'remote matter' (as Subtle terms it). They were differentiated in form by the four basic qualities of heat, cold, moisture and dryness as they in turn combined in and were expressed by the four elements, earth, air, fire and water. The word *element* in this system denoted not a substance (as in modern science) but a combination of qualities, as the diagram makes clear.

FIRE

hot   dry

AIR   **EARTH**

moist   cold

WATER

Thus fire was hot and dry, earth dry and cold, water cold and moist, air moist and hot. Predominance in the mixture of these elements determined the form of physical bodies, and the circularity of the relationship between the elements made transmutation possible: thus water's combination of cold and moisture could be shifted towards air's combination of heat and moisture as it boiled away into steam. Furthermore, transmutation from less perfect to more perfect bodies was enabled by the mixture of elements. Instability and imperfection were caused by unequal mixtures of the elements, and, although absolute perfection was not considered possible in the sublunary world, perfection could be approached in substances formed by more equally balanced mixtures of the elements. Gold was thought to be the most perfect substance, and the alchemist sought to make it by altering the elemental qualities present in base metals.

In practice, according to Geber and his followers, this meant the treatment of the two constituents of metals, mercury and sulphur. These were not the substances as they are found in nature, but rather the names given to essences or principles that inform metals: thus sulphur was the principle of combustibility or rusting, and mercury that of fluidity, the ability to melt and fuse. The purification of these principles as they exist in base metals could produce gold and, in their quintessence, the philosopher's stone itself. Some authorities identified the essence of mercury, 'the mercury of the philosophers', which had been refined of all impurities present in the natural metal, with the *prima materia*. The philosopher's stone was by the same token some refined principle of sulphur: as the 'white elixir' it would transmute mercury into silver, and in its yellow or red form it would produce gold.

There were numerous variations upon this theory, the most influential in the sixteenth century being that of Paracelsus (1493–1541), who proposed that the seven metals were composed of three, and not two, principles, his so-called *tria prima*, mercury, sulphur and salt. In one of the analogies with which alchemy abounds, he called mercury the spirit, salt the body, and sulphur the soul that united these two contraries in metals, and bound them into one essence.

The processes of the alchemical laboratory were often described in such anthropomorphic metaphors, moral, religious, sexual and social: mercury and sulphur were thought of as male and female principles, and the consummation of the alchemical process as a 'marriage'; 'base' metals were 'ennobled'; 'sick' substances were 'cured' by the stone; metals were turned into gold by being 'killed' and 'resurrected'. The 'vexations and the martyrizations / Of metals' and their 'mortification' and 'vivification' discussed by Face and Subtle (II.v.20 ff.) are typical. Astrological metaphors, implying an ascent from the corrupt sublunary to the increasingly pure spheres of Ptolomaic cosmography, were also commonly employed, turning upon the identification of the seven metals with the seven stars: gold (sun), silver (moon), copper (Venus), tin (Jupiter), iron (Mars), quicksilver (Mercury) and lead (Saturn). Such language linked the technical concerns of the laboratory to the fundamentals of philosophy, religion and cosmology. The dominance of analogy in alchemical thought meant that the metallurgical and medical properties of the stone or elixir could be seen as ultimately the same thing, and expressions of a striving towards perfection implicit in the whole of creation.

On the analogy with the conception, gestation and birth of animals, or the growth of plants, the development of minerals in the earth was thought of as an immensely slow organic process that could be speeded up in the laboratory. Practically, the alchemist sought to loosen the elemental composition of his materials by driving them through the cycle of heat, dryness, cold and moisture, with the aim of removing impurities. His apparatus was principally concerned with repeated combustion, solution, distillation and sublimation, and the climax of the work, 'the projection', involved sealing the purified materials in the vessel of Hermes, sometimes called the 'philosopher's egg' (on the analogy with birds' eggs hatching new life), and heating it in the athanor (furnace). The resulting sequence of colours – black, white, yellow and red (or purple) – indicated the work's progress to perfection.

A NOTE ON THE TEXT

The Alchemist was printed twice in Jonson's lifetime, as a Quarto in 1612 and in the Folio edition of Jonson's *Works* of

1616. There was a second Folio, published posthumously in 1640. Following the principles established by Herford and the Simpsons in their great edition of 1937, the text of this edition is closely based on that found in the 1616 Folio, and includes the Quarto's preface 'To the Reader', which was not reprinted in the Folio. The author carefully prepared the Folio for the press, and *The Alchemist* was probably set from a copy of the Quarto containing his corrections and amendments. Jonson revised the punctuation, making it heavier and more consistent than in the Quarto, and made some minor typographical alterations. There are a few small deletions, substitutions and rewritings, and, where the Quarto contained only one stage direction, there are a number in the Folio. Oaths naming the Deity and other overt blasphemies were toned down, no doubt reflecting a more active censorship.

The spelling, punctuation and typography of this edition have all been modernized with the aim of producing a text readily accessible to the modern reader. Metrical elisions have been retained, with one exception. Modern pronunciation makes the elision of the participial suffix *-ed* to *-'d* unnecessary to preserve metre. In the few cases where Jonson requires the accenting of the suffix, this is marked in the text. Such elisions as *y'are*, *yo'are*, *h'is* and *'hem* have been regularized in accordance with modern usage, and *yo'were* and *y'were*, lacking a modern equivalent, have been printed in the latter form. *And* and *an'*, where they mean 'if', have been regularized as *and*.

Jonson divided his play in the manner of classical drama, at the entry of each new important character, and not in the way natural to the theatre, at the end of each cleared-stage scene. Thus, although Act I is really one continuous scene, Jonson divides it into four. He also follows classical practice in using block entries, putting the names of all the participating characters at the head of the scene. The scene divisions have been retained on the grounds that they have become the basis of standard reference to the play, but block entries have been broken up so that characters' names appear at their entries and exits. The speech prefix of the first speaker in each scene, unnecessary under Jonson's system, has been supplied. Stage directions have been regularized and expanded where necessary, often incorporating the suggestions of previous editors such as Gifford (1816). Square brackets enclose material supplied by the editor.

THE ALCHEMIST
Ben Jonson

TO THE LADY MOST DESERVING HER NAME,
AND BLOOD: MARY, LA[DY] WROTH

MADAM,
In the age of sacrifices, the truth of religion was not in the
greatness and fat of the offerings, but in the devotion and
zeal of the sacrificers; else what could a handful of gums
have done in the sight of a hecatomb? Or how might I
appear at this altar, except with those affections that no
less love the light and witness than they have the conscience of your virtue? If what I offer bear an acceptable
odour and hold the first strength, it is your value of it
which remembers where, when, and to whom it was   10
kindled. Otherwise, as the times are, there comes rarely
forth that thing so full of authority or example, but by
assiduity and custom grows less and loses. This, yet safe
in your judgement (which is a SIDNEY's), is forbidden to
speak more lest it talk or look like one of the ambitious
faces of the time; who, the more they paint, are the less
themselves.

> Your La[dyship's]
> true honourer,
> BEN. JONSON   20

If thou beest more, thou art an understander, and then I
trust thee. If thou art one that takest up, and but a
pretender, beware at what hands thou receivest thy commodity; for thou wert never more fair in the way to be
cozened than (in this age) in poetry, especially in plays;
wherein now the concupiscence of dances and antics so
reigneth, as to run away from nature and be afraid of her
is the only point of art that tickles the spectators. But
how out of purpose and place do I name art, when the professors are grown so obstinate contemners of it, and pre-   10
sumers on their own naturals, as they are deriders of all
diligence that way; and by simple mocking at the terms,
when they understand not the things, think to get off
wittily with their ignorance. Nay, they are esteemed the
more learned and sufficient for this by the many, through
their excellent vice of judgement. For they commend
writers as they do fencers or wrestlers; who, if they come
in robustiously, and put for it with a great deal of
violence, are received for the braver fellows, when many
times their own rudeness is the cause of their disgrace,   20
and a little touch of their adversary gives all that
boisterous force the foil. I deny not but that these men,
who always seek to do more than enough, may some
time happen on something that is good and great, but
very seldom; and when it comes it doth not recompense
the rest of their ill. It sticks out perhaps and is more
eminent because all is sordid and vile about it, as lights
are more discerned in a thick darkness than a faint sha-
dow. I speak not this out of a hope to do good on any
man against nis will; for I know, if it were put to the   30
question of theirs and mine, the worse would find more

suffrages because the most favour common errors. But I give thee this warning: that there is a great difference between those that (to gain the opinion of copy) utter all they can, however unfitly, and those that use election and a mean. For it is only the disease of the unskilful to think rude things greater than polished, or scattered more numerous than composed.

THE PERSONS OF THE PLAY

SUBTLE, *the alchemist*
FACE, *the housekeeper*
DOLL COMMON, *their colleague*
DAPPER, *a clerk*
DRUGGER, *a tobacco-man*
LOVEWIT, *[the] master of the house*
EPICURE MAMMON, *a knight*
SURLY, *a gamester*
TRIBULATION, *a pastor of Amsterdam*
ANANIAS, *a deacon there*   10
KASTRIL, *the angry boy*
DAME PLIANT, *his sister: a widow*

Neighbours
   Officers
      Mutes

THE SCENE
London

THE ARGUMENT

The sickness hot, a master quit, for fear,
His house in town, and left one servant there.
Ease him corrupted, and gave means to know
A cheater and his punk; who, now brought low,
Leaving their narrow practice, were become
Coz'ners at large; and only wanting some
House to set up, with him they here contract
Each for a share, and all begin to act.
Much company they draw, and much abuse,
In casting figures, telling fortunes, news,   10
Selling of flies, flat bawdry, with the stone;
Till it, and they, and all in fume are gone.

PROLOGUE

Fortune, that favours fools, these two short hours
   We wish away, both for your sakes and ours,
Judging Spectators; and desire in place
   To th'author justice, to ourselves but grace.
Our scene is London, 'cause we would make known
   No country's mirth is better than our own.
No clime breeds better matter for your whore,
   Bawd, squire, impostor, many persons more;
Whose manners, now called humours, feed the stage,
   And which have still been subject for the rage   10
Or spleen of comic writers. Though this pen
   Did never aim to grieve, but better men,
Howe'er the age he lives in doth endure
   The vices that she breeds, above their cure.
But when the wholesome remedies are sweet,
   And, in their working, gain and profit meet,
He hopes to find no spirit so much diseased,
   But will, with such fair correctives, be pleased.
For here he doth not fear who can apply.
   If there be any that will sit so nigh   20
Unto the stream to look what it doth run,
   They shall find things they'd think, or wish, were done;
They are so natural follies, but so shown,
   As even the doers may see, and yet not own.

THE ALCHEMIST

ACT I

SCENE I

[*Enter*] FACE, SUBTLE [*and*] DOLL COMMON.

[*Face.*] Believe't, I will.

Sub.   Thy worst. I fart at thee.

Doll. Ha' you your wits? Why, gentlemen! For love –

Face. Sirrah, I'll strip you –

Sub.   What to do? Lick figs
   Out at my –

Face.   Rogue, rogue, out of all your sleights.

Doll. Nay, look ye! Sovereign, General, are you madmen?

Sub. O, let the wild sheep loose. I'll gum your silks
   With good strong water, and you come.

Doll.   Will you have
   The neighbours hear you? Will you betray all?
   Hark, I hear somebody.

Face.   Sirrah –

Sub.   I shall mar
   All that the tailor has made, if you approach.   10

Face. You most notorious whelp, you insolent slave.
   Dare you do this?

Sub.   Yes faith, yes faith.

Face.   Why! Who
    Am I, my mongrel? Who am I?
Sub.   I'll tell you,
    Since you know not yourself –
Face.   Speak lower, rogue.
Sub. Yes, You were once (time's not long past) the good,
    Honest, plain livery-three-pound-thrum that kept
    Your master's worship's house here in the Friars
    For the vacations –
Face.   Will you be so loud?
Sub. Since, by my means, translated suburb-captain.
Face. By your means, Doctor Dog?
Sub.   Within man's memory,   20
    All this I speak of.
Face.   Why, I pray you, have I
    Been countenanced by you? Or you by me?
    Do but collect, sir, where I met you first.
Sub. I do not hear well.
Face.   Not of this, I think it.
    But I shall put you in mind, sir: at Pie Corner,
    Taking your meal of steam in from cooks' stalls,
    Where, like the father of hunger, you did walk
    Piteously costive, with your pinched-horn nose,
    And your complexion of the Roman wash,
    Stuck full of black and melancholic worms,   30
    Like powder corns shot at th'artillery yard.
Sub. I wish you could advance your voice a little.
Face. When you went pinned up in the several rags
    You'd raked and picked from dunghills before day,
    Your feet in mouldy slippers for your kibes,
    A felt of rug, and a thin threaden cloak
    That scarce would cover your no-buttocks –
Sub.   So, sir!
Face. When all your alchemy and your algebra,
    Your minerals, vegetals, and animals,
    Your conjuring, coz'ning, and your dozen of trades,   40
    Could not relieve your corpse with so much linen

    Would make you tinder, but to see a fire;
    I ga' you count'nance, credit for your coals,
    Your stills, your glasses, your materials;
    Built you a furnace, drew you customers,
    Advanced all your black arts; lent you, beside,
    A house to practise in –
Sub.   Your master's house?
Face. Where you have studied the more thriving skill
    Of bawdry, since.
Sub.   Yes, in your master's house.
    You and the rats here kept possession.   50
    Make it not strange. I know y'were one could keep
    The butt'ry-hatch still locked, and save the chippings,
    Sell the dole beer to *aqua-vitae* men,
    The which, together with your Christmas vails
    At post and pair, your letting out of counters,
    Made you a pretty stock, some twenty marks,
    And gave you credit to converse with cobwebs
    Here, since your mistress' death hath broke up house.
Face. You might talk softlier, rascal.
Sub.   No, you scarab,
    I'll thunder you in pieces. I will teach you   60
    How to beware to tempt a fury again,
    That carries tempest in his hand and voice.
Face. The place has made you valiant.
Sub.   No, your clothes.
    Thou vermin, have I ta'en thee out of dung,
    So poor, so wretched, when no living thing
    Would keep thee company but a spider, or worse?
    Raised thee from brooms, and dust, and wat'ring pots?
    Sublimed thee, and exalted thee, and fixed thee
    I' the third region, called our state of grace?
    Wrought thee to spirit, to quintessence, with pains   70
    Would twice have won me the philosopher's work?
    Put thee in words and fashion? Made thee fit
    For more than ordinary fellowships?
    Giv'n thee thy oaths, thy quarrelling dimensions?

Thy rules to cheat at horse-race, cock-pit, cards,
Dice, or whatever gallant tincture else?
Made thee a second in mine own great art?
And have I this for thank? Do you rebel?
Do you fly out i' the projection?
Would you be gone now?

Doll.   Gentlemen, what mean you?   80
Will you mar all?

Sub.   Slave, thou hadst had no name –

Doll. Will you undo yourselves with civil war?

Sub. Never been known, past *equi clibanum*,
The heat of horse-dung, underground, in cellars,
Or an alehouse darker than deaf John's; been lost
To all mankind but laundresses and tapsters,
Had not I been.

Doll.   Do you know who hears you, Sovereign?

Face. Sirrah –

Doll.   Nay, General, I thought you were civil –

Face. I shall turn desperate if you grow thus loud.

Sub. And hang thyself, I care not.

Face.   Hang thee, collier,   90
And all thy pots and pans, in picture, I will,
Since thou hast moved me –

Doll.   O, this'll o'erthrow all.

Face. Write thee up bawd in Paul's: have all thy tricks
Of coz'ning with a hollow coal, dust, scrapings,
Searching for things lost, with a sieve and shears,
Erecting figures in your rows of houses,
And taking in of shadows with a glass,
Told in red letters; and a face cut for thee,
Worse than Gamaliel Ratsey's.

Doll.   Are you sound?
Ha' you your senses, masters?

Face.   I will have   100
A book, but barely reckoning thy impostures,
Shall prove a true philosopher's stone to printers.

Sub. Away, you trencher-rascal!

Face.   Out, you dog-leech,
     The vomit of all prisons –
Doll.   Will you be
     Your own destructions, gentlemen?
Face.   Still spewed out
     For lying too heavy o' the basket.
Sub.   Cheater!
Face.   Bawd!
Sub. Cowherd!
Face.   Conjuror!
Sub.   Cutpurse!
Face.   Witch!
Doll.   O me!
     We are ruined! Lost! Ha' you no more regard
     To your reputations? Where's your judgement? 'Slight,
     Have yet some care of me, o' your republic –   110
Face. Away this brach! I'll bring thee, rogue, within
     The statute of sorcery, *tricesimo tertio*
     Of Harry the eight; ay, and perhaps thy neck
     Within a noose, for laund'ring gold and barbing it.
Doll. You'll bring your head within a coxcomb, will you?
          She catcheth out Face's sword and breaks Subtle's glass.
     And you, sir, with you menstrue, gather it up.
     'Sdeath, you abominable pair of stinkards,
     Leave off your barking, and grow one again,
     Or, by the light that shines, I'll cut your throats.
     I'll not be made a prey unto the marshal   120
     For ne'er a snarling dog-bolt o' you both.
     Ha' you together cozened all this while,
     And all the world, and shall it now be said
     You've made most courteous shift to cozen yourselves?
     [*To Face*] You will accuse him? You will bring him in
     Within the statute? Who shall take your word?
     A whoreson, upstart, apocryphal captain,
     Whom not a Puritan in Blackfriars will trust
     So much as for a feather! [*To Subtle*] And you, too,
     Will give the cause, forsooth? You will insult,   130

And claim a primacy in the divisions?
You must be chief? As if you only had
The powder to project with, and the work
Were not begun out of equality?
The venture tripartite? All things in common?
Without priority? 'Sdeath, you perpetual curs,
Fall to your couples again, and cozen kindly
And heartily and lovingly as you should,
And lose not the beginning of a term,
Or, by this hand, I shall grow factious too,   140
And take my part, and quit you.
Face.   'Tis his fault:
    He ever murmurs, and objects his pains,
    And says the weight of all lies upon him.
Sub. Why, so it does.
Doll.   How does it? Do not we
    Sustain our parts?
Sub.   Yes, but they are not equal.
Doll. Why, if your part exceed today, I hope
    Ours may tomorrow match it.
Sub.   Ay, they may.
Doll. May, murmuring mastiff? Ay, and do. Death on me!
    [*To Face*] Help me to throttle him.
Sub.   Dorothy,
    Mistress Dorothy!
    'Ods precious, I'll do anything! What do you mean?   150
Doll. Because o' your fermentation and cibation?
Sub. Not I, by heaven –
Doll.   Your *Sol* and *Luna* – [*To Face*]
    help me.
Sub. Would I were hanged then. I'll conform myself.
Doll. Will you, sir? Do so then, and quickly: swear.
Sub. What should I swear?
Doll.   To leave your faction, sir.
    And labour kindly in the common work.
Sub. Let me not breathe if I meant aught beside.
    I only used those speeches as a spur
    To him.

Doll.   I hope we need no spurs, sir. Do we?
Face. 'Slid, prove today who shall shark best.
Sub.   Agreed.   160
Doll. Yes, and work close and friendly.
Sub.   'Slight, the knot
   Shall grow the stronger for this breach, with me.
Doll. Why so, my good baboons! Shall we go make
   A sort of sober, scurvy, precise neighbours
   That scarce have smiled twice sin' the king came in,
   A feast of laughter at our follies? Rascals,
   Would run themselves from breath to see me ride,
   Or you t'have but a hole to thrust your heads in,
   For which you should pay ear-rent? No, agree;
   And may Don Provost ride a-feasting long,   170
   In his old velvet jerkin and stained scarves,
   My noble Sovereign and worthy General,
   Ere we contribute a new crewel garter
   To his most worsted worship.
Sub.   Royal Doll!
   Spoken like Claridiana, and thyself!
Face. For which at supper thou shalt sit in triumph,
   And not be styled Doll Common, but Doll Proper,
   Doll Singular; the longest cut at night
   Shall draw thee for his Doll Particular.
Sub. Who's that? One rings. To the window, Doll. 'Pray
      heav'n   180
   The master do not trouble us this quarter.
Face. O, fear not him. While there dies one a week
   O' the plague, he's safe from thinking toward London.
   Beside, he's busy at his hop-yards now;
   I had a letter from him. If he do,
   He'll send such word for airing of the house
   As you shall have sufficient time to quit it:
   Though we break up a fortnight, 'tis no matter.
Sub. Who is it, Doll?
Doll.   A fine young quodling.
Face.   O,

My lawyer's clerk, I lighted on last night　　　　　190
In Holborn, at the Dagger. He would have
(I told you of him) a familiar
To rifle with at horses, and win cups.
Doll. O, let him in.
Sub.　　　　　　Stay. Who shall do't?
Face.　　　　　　　　　Get you
Your robes on. I will meet him, as going out.
Doll. And what shall I do?
Face.　　　　　　Not be seen, away.　　*[Exit Doll.]*
Seem you very reserved.
Sub.　　　　　　Enough.
Face.　　　　　　　　God be wi' you, sir.
I pray you, let him know that I was here.
His name is Dapper. I would gladly have stayed, but –

SCENE II

[*Enter*] DAPPER.

[*Dap.*] Captain, I am here.
Face.　　　　　Who's that? He's come, I think,
　　Doctor.
Good faith, sir, I was going away.
Dap.　　　　　　　In truth,
I'm very sorry, Captain.
Face.　　　　　　But I thought
Sure I should meet you.
Dap.　　　　　　Ay, I'm very glad.
I had a scurvy writ or two to make,
And I had lent my watch last night to one
That dines today at the sheriff's, and so was robbed
Of my pass-time. Is this the cunning-man?
Face. This is his worship.
Dap.　　　　　Is he a doctor?

Face.   Yes.
Dap. And ha' you broke with him, Captain?
Face.   Ay.
Dap.   And how?   10
Face. Faith, he does make the matter, sir, so dainty,
    I know not what to say –
Dap.   Not so, good Captain!
Face. Would I were fairly rid on't, believe me.
Dap. Nay, now you grieve me, sir. Why should you wish so?
    I dare assure you, I'll not be ungrateful.
Face. I cannot think you will, sir. But the law
    Is such a thing – and then, he says, Read's matter
    Falling so lately –
Dap.   Read? He was an ass,
    And dealt, sir, with a fool.
Face.   It was a clerk, sir.
Dap. A clerk?
Face.   Nay, hear me, sir, you know the law   20
    Better, I think –
Dap.   I should, sir, and the danger.
    You know I showed the statute to you.
Face.   You did so.
Dap. And will I tell, then? By this hand of flesh,
    Would it might never write good court-hand more
    If I discover. What do you think of me,
    That I am a *chiaus*?
Face.   What's that?
Dap.   The Turk was, here –
    As one would say, 'Do you think I am a Turk?'
Face. I'll tell the Doctor so.
Dap.   Do, good sweet Captain.
Face. Come, noble Doctor, 'pray thee, let's prevail,
    This is the gentleman, and he is no *chiaus*.   30
Sub. Captain, I have returned you all my answer.
    I would do much, sir, for your love – but this
    I neither may, nor can.
Face.   Tut, do not say so.

You deal now with a noble fellow, Doctor.
One that will thank you richly, and he's no *chiaus*:
Let that, sir, move you.
Sub.   'Pray you, forbear –
Face.   He has
Four angels here –
Sub.   You do me wrong, good sir.
Face. Doctor, wherein? To tempt you with these spirits?
Sub. To tempt my art and love, sir, to my peril.
'Fore heav'n, I scarce can think you are my friend,   40
That so would draw me to apparent danger.
Face. I draw you? A horse draw you, and a halter,
You, and your flies together –
Dap.   Nay, good Captain.
Face. That know no difference of men.
Sub.   Good words, sir.
Face. Good deeds, sir, Doctor Dog's-meat. 'Slight, I bring you
No cheating Clim o' the Cloughs or Claribels
That look as big as five-and-fifty and flush,
And spit out secrets like hot custard –
Dap.   Captain.
Face. Nor any melancholic under-scribe
Shall tell the vicar; but a special gentle   50
That is the heir to forty marks a year,
Consorts with the small poets of the time,
Is the sole hope of his old grandmother;
That knows the law, and writes you six fair hands,
Is a fine clerk, and has his ciph'ring perfect;
Will take his oath o' the Greek Xenophon,
If need be, in his pocket; and can court
His mistress out of Ovid.
Dap.   Nay, dear Captain.
Face. Did you not tell me so?
Dap.   Yes, but I'd ha' you
Use Master Doctor with some more respect.   60
Face. Hang him, proud stag, with his broad velvet head.
But for your sake, I'd choke ere I would change

    An article of breath with such a puck-fist –
    Come let's be gone.
Sub.   'Pray you, le' me speak with you.
Dap. His worship calls you, Captain.
Face.   I am sorry
    I e'er embarked myself in such a business.
Dap. Nay, good sir. He did call you.
Face.   Will he take, then?
Sub. First, hear me –
Face.   Not a syllable, 'less you take.
Sub. 'Pray ye, sir –
Face.   Upon no terms but an *assumpsit*.
Sub. Your humour must be law.   *He takes the money*.
Face.   Why now, sir, talk.   70
    Now, I dare hear you with mine honour. Speak.
    So may this gentleman too.
Sub   Why, sir –
Face.   No whisp'ring.
Sub. 'Fore heav'n, you do not apprehend the loss
    You do yourself in this.
Face.   Wherein? For what?
Sub. Marry, to be so importunate for one
    That, when he has it, will undo you all:
    He'll win up all the money i' the town.
Face. How!
Sub.   Yes. And blow up gamester after gamester,
    As they do crackers in a puppet-play.
    If I do give him a familiar,   80
    Give you him all you play for; never set him,
    For he will have it.
Face.   You're mistaken, Doctor.
    Why, he does ask one but for cups and horses,
    A rifling fly; none o' your great familiars.
Dap. Yes, Captain, I would have it for all games.
Sub. I told you so.
Face.   'Slight, that's a new business!
    I understood you, a tame bird, to fly

Twice in a term or so, on Friday nights
When you had left the office, for a nag
Of forty or fifty shillings.

Dap.   Ay, 'tis true, sir,   90
But I do think, now, I shall leave the law,
And therefore –

Face.   Why, this changes quite the case!
Do you think that I dare move him?

Dap.   If you please, sir,
All's one to him, I see.

Face.   What! For that money?
I cannot with my conscience. Nor should you
Make the request, methinks.

Dap.   No, sir, I mean
To add consideration.

Face.   Why then, sir,
I'll try. Say that it were for all games, Doctor?

Sub. I say, then, not a mouth shall eat for him
At any ordinary, but o' the score,   100
That is a gaming mouth, conceive me.

Face.   Indeed!

Sub.   He'll draw you all the treasure of the realm,
If it be set him.

Face.   Speak you this from art?

Sub. Ay, sir, and reason too, the ground of art.
He's o' the only best complexion
The Queen of Fairy loves.

Face.   What! Is he!

Sub.   Peace.
He'll overhear you. Sir, should she but see him –

Face. What?

Sub.   Do not you tell him.

Face.   Will he win at cards too?

Sub. The spirits of dead Holland, living Isaac,
You'd swear were in him; such a vigorous luck   110
As cannot be resisted. 'Slight, he'll put
Six o' your gallants to a cloak, indeed.

Face. A strange success, that some man shall be born to!

Sub. He hears you, man –

Dap.   Sir, I'll not be ingrateful.

Face. Faith, I have a confidence in his good nature:

You hear, he says he will not be ingrateful.

Sub. Why, as you please; my venture follows yours.

Face. Troth, do it, Doctor. Think him trusty, and make him.

He may make us both happy in an hour:

Win some five thousand pound, and send us two on't.   120

Dap. Believe it, and I will, sir.

Face.   And you shall, sir.

You have heard all?   *Face takes him aside*.

Dap.   No, what was't? Nothing, I, sir.

Face. Nothing?

Dap.   A little, sir.

Face.   Well, a rare star

Reigned at your birth.

Dap.   At mine, sir? No.

Face.   The Doctor

Swears that you are –

Sub.   Nay, Captain, you'll tell all, now.

Face. Allied to the Queen of Fairy.

Dap.   Who? That I am?

Believe it, no such matter –

Face.   Yes, and that

Y'were born with a caul o' your head.

Dap.   Who says so?

Face.   Come.

You know it well enough, though you dissemble it.

Dap. I' fac, I do not. You are mistaken.

Face.   How!   130

Swear by your fac? And in a thing so known

Unto the Doctor? How shall we, sir, trust you

I' the other matter? Can we ever think,

When you have won five or six thousand pound,

You'll send us shares in't, by this rate?

Dap.   By Jove, sir,

I'll win ten thousand pound, and send you half.
I' fac's no oath.
Sub.   No, no, he did but jest.
Face. Go to. Go, thank the Doctor. He's your friend
  To take it so.
Dap.   I thank his worship.
Face.   So?
  Another angel.
Dap.   Must I?
Face.   Must you? 'Slight,   140
  What else is thanks? Will you be trivial? Doctor,
  When must he come for his familiar?
Dap. Shall I not ha' it with me?
Sub.   O, good sir!
  There must a world of ceremonies pass:
  You must be bathed and fumigated, first.
  Besides, the Queen of Fairy does not rise
  Till it be noon.
Face.   Not if she danced tonight.
Sub. And she must bless it.
Face.   Did you never see
  Her royal Grace, yet?
Dap.   Whom?
Face.   Your aunt of Fairy?
Sub. Not since she kissed him in the cradle, Captain,   150
  I can resolve you that.
Face.   Well, see her Grace,
  Whate'er it cost you, for a thing that I know!
  It will be somewhat hard to compass; but,
  However, see her. You are made, believe it,
  If you can see her. Her Grace is a lone woman,
  And very rich, and if she take a fancy,
  She will do strange things. See her, at any hand.
  'Slid, she may hap to leave you all she has!
  It is the Doctor's fear.
Dap.   How will't be done, then?
Face. Let me alone, take you no thought. Do you   160
  But say to me, 'Captain, I'll see her Grace'.

Dap. Captain, I'll see her Grace.   *One knocks without.*
Face.   Enough.
Sub.   Who's there?
    Anon. [*Aside to Face*] Conduct him forth by the back
      way –
    Sir, against one o'clock, prepare yourself.
    Till when you must be fasting; only, take
    Three drops of vinegar in at your nose,
    Two at your mouth, and one at either ear;
    Then bathe your fingers' ends and wash your eyes,
    To sharpen your five senses; and cry 'hum'
    Thrice, and then 'buzz' as often; and then, come.   170
Face. Can you remember this?
Dap.   I warrant you.
Face. Well then, away. 'Tis but your bestowing
    Some twenty nobles 'mong her Grace's servants;
    And put on a clean shirt: you do not know
    What grace her Grace may do you in clean linen.
                              [Exeunt Dapper and Face.]

SCENE III

[*Enter*] DRUGGER.

[*Sub.*] Come in. – Good wives, I pray you forbear me now.
    Troth, I can do you no good till afternoon. –
    What is your name, say you? Abel Drugger?
Dru.   Yes, sir.
Sub. A seller of tobacco?
Dru.   Yes, sir.
Sub.   'Umh.
    Free of the Grocers?
Dru.   Ay, and't please you.
Sub.   Well –
    Your business, Abel?
Dru.   This, and't please your worship:

I am a young beginner, and am building
Of a new shop, and't like your worship, just
At corner of a street – here's the plot on't –
And I would know by art, sir, of your worship,   10
Which way I should make my door, by necromancy,
And where my shelves, and which should be for boxes,
And which for pots. I would be glad to thrive, sir.
And I was wished to your worship by a gentleman,
One Captain Face, that says you know men's planets,
And their good angels, and their bad.
Sub.   I do.
     If I do see 'em –

               [*Enter*] FACE.

Face.   What! My honest Abel?
     Thou art well met, here!
Dru.   Troth, sir, I was speaking,
     Just as your worship came here, of your worship.
     I pray you, speak for me to Master Doctor.   20
Face. He shall do anything. Doctor, do you hear?
     This is my friend, Abel, an honest fellow;
     He lets me have good tobacco, and he does not
     Sophisticate it with sack-lees or oil,
     Nor washes it in muscadel and grains,
     Nor buries it in gravel underground,
     Wrapped up in greasy leather or pissed clouts,
     But keeps it in fine lily-pots that, opened,
     Smell like conserve of roses or French beans.
     He has his maple block, his silver tongs,   30
     Winchester pipes, and fire of juniper:
     A neat, spruce-honest fellow, and no goldsmith.
Sub. He's a fortunate fellow, that I am sure on –
Face. Already, sir, ha' you found it? Lo thee, Abel!
Sub. And in right way toward riches –
Face.   Sir!
Sub.   This summer
     He will be of the clothing of his company,

And next spring, called to the scarlet. Spend what he can.

Face. What, and so little beard?

Sub.   Sir, you must think,
He may have a receipt to make hair come.
But he'll be wise, preserve his youth, and fine for't: 40
His fortune looks for him another way.

Face. 'Slid, Doctor, how canst thou know this so soon?
I'm amused at that!

Sub.   By a rule, Captain,
In metoposcopy, which I do work by:
A certain star i' the forehead, which you see not.
Your chestnut or your olive-coloured face
Does never fail, and your long ear doth promise.
I knew't by certain spots too in his teeth,
And on the nail of his mercurial finger.

Face. Which finger's that?

Sub.   His little finger. Look.   50
Y'were born upon a Wednesday?

Dru.   Yes, indeed, sir.

Sub. The thumb, in chiromanty, we give Venus;
The forefinger to Jove; the midst to Saturn;
The ring to *Sol*; the least to Mercury,
Who was the lord, sir, of his horoscope,
His house of life being Libra; which foreshowed
He should be a merchant, and should trade with balance.

Face. Why, this is strange! Is't not, honest Nab?

Sub. There is a ship now coming from Ormus,
That shall yield him such a commodity   60
Of drugs – This is the west, and this the south?

                              [*Examining Drugger's plans.*]

Dru. Yes, sir.

Sub.   And those are your two sides?

Dru.   Ay, sir.

Sub. Make me your door, then, south; your broad side, west;
And on the east side of your shop, aloft,
Write *Mathlai, Tarmiel* and *Baraborat*;
Upon the north part, *Rael, Velel, Thiel.*

   They are the names of those mercurial spirits
   That do fright flies from boxes.
Dru.   Yes, sir.
Sub.   And
   Beneath your threshold, bury me a lodestone
   To draw in gallants that wear spurs. The rest,   70
   They'll seem to follow.
Face.   That's a secret, Nab!
Sub. And on your stall, a puppet with a vice,
   And a court fucus, to call city dames.
   You shall deal much with minerals.
Dru.   Sir, I have
   At home, already –
Sub.   Ay, I know, you have arsenic,
   Vitriol, sal-tartar, argaile, alkali,
   Cinoper: I know all. This fellow, Captain,
   Will come in time to be a great distiller,
   And give a say (I will not say directly,
   But very fair) at the philosopher's stone.   80
Face. Why, how now, Abel! Is this true?
Dru.   Good Captain,
   What must I give?
Face.   Nay, I'll not counsel thee.
   Thou hear'st what wealth (he says, spend what thou canst)
   Th'art like to come to.
Dru.   I would gi' him a crown.
Face. A crown! And toward such a fortune? Heart,
   Thou shalt rather gi' him thy shop. No gold about thee?
Dru. Yes, I have a portague I ha' kept this half year.
Face. Out on thee, Nab! 'Slight, there was such an offer –
   'Shalt keep't no longer. I'll gi't him for thee?
   Doctor, Nab prays your worship to drink this, and
    swears   90
   He will appear more grateful, as your skill
   Does raise him in the world.
Dru.   I would entreat
   Another favour of his worship.

Face.   What is't, Nab?

Dru. But to look over, sir, my almanac,
And cross out my ill-days, that I may neither
Bargain nor trust upon them.

Face.   That he shall, Nab.
Leave it; it shall be done 'gainst afternoon.

Sub. And a direction for his shelves.

Face.   Now, Nab?
Art thou well pleased, Nab?

Dru.   Thank, sir, both your
worships.

Face.   Away.   [*Exit Drugger.*]
Why, now, you smoky persecutor of nature!   100
Now do you see that something's to be done
Besides your beech-coal and your cor'sive waters,
Your crosslets, crucibles and cucurbites?
You must have stuff brought home to you to work on!
And yet you think I am at no expense
In searching out these veins, then following 'em,
Then trying 'em out. 'Fore God, my intelligence
Costs me more money than my share oft comes to,
In these rare works.

Sub.   You are pleasant, sir. How now?

SCENE IV

[*Enter*] DOLL.

Sub. What says my dainty Dolkin?

Doll.   Yonder fishwife
Will not away. And there's your giantess,
The bawd of Lambeth.

Sub.   Heart, I cannot speak with 'em.

Doll. Not afore night, I have told 'em, in a voice
Thorough the trunk, like one of your familiars.
But I have spied Sir Epicure Mammon –

Sub.   Where?

Doll. Coming along at far end of the lane,
    Slow of his feet, but earnest of his tongue
    To one that's with him.

Sub.   Face, go you and shift. [*Exit Face.*]
    Doll, you must presently make ready too.   10

Doll. Why, what's the matter?

Sub.   O, I did look for him
    With the sun's rising: 'marvel he could sleep!
    This is the day I am to perfect for him
    The *magisterium*, our great work, the stone,
    And yield it, made, into his hands; of which
    He has this month talked as he were possessed.
    And now he's dealing pieces on't away.
    Methinks I see him entering ordinaries,
    Dispensing for the pox; and plaguy houses,
    Reaching his dose; walking Moorfields for lepers;   20
    And off'ring citizens' wives pomander-bracelets
    As his preservative, made of the elixir;
    Searching the spital to make old bawds young;
    And the highways for beggars to make rich;
    I see no end of his labours. He will make
    Nature ashamed of her long sleep, when art,
    Who's but a stepdame, shall do more than she,
    In her best love to mankind, ever could.
    If his dream last, he'll turn the age to gold.   [*Exeunt.*]

ACT II

SCENE I

[*Enter*] MAMMON [*and*] SURLY.

Mam. Come on, sir. Now you set your foot on shore
In *novo orbe*; here's the rich Peru,
And there within, sir, are the golden mines,
Great Solomon's Ophir! He was sailing to't
Three years, but we have reached it in ten months.
This is the day wherein, to all my friends,
I will pronounce the happy word, 'Be rich'.
This day you shall be *spectatissimi*.
You shall no more deal with the hollow die
Or the frail card. No more be at charge of keeping   10
The livery-punk for the young heir that must
Seal at all hours in his shirt. No more,
If he deny, ha' him beaten to't, as he is
That brings him the commodity. No more
Shall thirst of satin, or the covetous hunger
Of velvet entrails for a rude-spun cloak,
To be displayed at Madam Augusta's, make
The sons of sword and hazard fall before
The golden calf, and on their knees, whole nights,
Commit idolatry with wine and trumpets,   20
Or go a-feasting after drum and ensign.
No more of this. You shall start up young viceroys,
And have your punks and punketees, my Surly.
And unto thee I speak it first, 'Be rich'.
Where is my Subtle, there? Within, ho!
[*Face.*] (*Within*)   Sir,

He'll come to you by and by.

Mam.   That's his fire-drake,
His lungs, his Zephyrus, he that puffs his coals
Till he firk nature up in her own centre.
You are not faithful, sir. This night I'll change
All that is metal in thy house to gold.   30
And early in the morning will I send
To all the plumbers and the pewterers,
And buy their tin and lead up; and to Lothbury,
For all the copper.

Sur.   What, and turn that too?

Mam. Yes, and I'll purchase Devonshire and Cornwall,
And make them perfect Indies! You admire now?

Sur. No, faith.

Mam.   But when you see th'effects of the great
      med'cine,
Of which one part projected on a hundred
Of Mercury, or Venus, or the Moon,
Shall turn it to as many of the Sun,   40
Nay, to a thousand, so *ad infinitum*,
You will believe me.

Sur.   Yes, when I see't, I will.
But if my eyes do cozen me so (and I
Giving 'em no occasion), sure, I'll have
A whore shall piss 'em out next day.

Mam.   Ha! Why?
Do you think I fable with you? I assure you,
He that has once the flower of the sun,
The perfect ruby, which we call elixir,
Not only can do that, but, by its virtue,
Can confer honour, love, respect, long life;   50
Give safety, valour, yea, and victory
To whom he will. In eight and twenty days
I'll make an old man of fourscore a child.

Sur. No doubt he's that already.

Mam.   Nay, I mean
Restore his years, renew him like an eagle

     To the fifth age; make him get sons and daughters,
     Young giants, as our philosophers have done
     (The ancient patriarchs afore the flood)
     But taking, once a week, on a knife's point,
     The quantity of a grain of mustard of it: 60
     Become stout Marses and beget young Cupids.
Sur. The decayed vestals of Pict-hatch would thank you,
     That keep the fire alive there.
Mam.   'Tis the secret
     Of nature naturized 'gainst all infections,
     Cures all diseases coming of all causes:
     A month's grief in a day, a year's in twelve,
     And of what age soever, in a month;
     Past all the doses of your drugging doctors.
     I'll undertake, withal, to fright the plague
     Out o' the kingdom in three months.
Sur.   And I'll   70
     Be bound, the players shall sing your praises then
     Without their poets.
Mam.   Sir, I'll do't. Meantime,
     I'll give away so much unto my man
     Shall serve th'whole city with preservative
     Weekly, each house his dose, and at the rate –
Sur. As he that built the waterwork does with water?
Mam. You are incredulous.
Sur.   Faith, I have a humour:
     I would not willingly be gulled. Your stone
     Cannot transmute me.
Mam.   Pertinax, Surly,
     Will you believe antiquity? Records?   80
     I'll show you a book where Moses and his sister
     And Solomon have written of the art;
     Ay, and a treatise penned by Adam –
Sur.   How!
Mam. O' the philosopher's stone, and in High Dutch.
Sur. Did Adam write, sir, in High Dutch?
Mam.   He did;

Which proves it was the primitive tongue.

Sur.   What paper?

Mam. On cedar board.

Sur.   O that indeed, they say,
     Will last 'gainst worms.

Mam.   'Tis like your Irish wood
     'Gainst cobwebs. I have a piece of Jason's fleece, too,
     Which was no other than a book of alchemy   90
     Writ in large sheepskin, a good fat ram-vellum.
     Such was Pythagoras' thigh, Pandora's tub,
     And all that fable of Medea's charms,
     The manner of our work: the bulls, our furnace,
     Still breathing fire; our *argent-vive*, the dragon;
     The dragon's teeth, mercury sublimate
     That keeps the whiteness, hardness, and the biting;
     And they are gathered into Jason's helm
     (Th'alembic) and then sowed in Mars his field,
     And thence sublimed so often till they are fixed.   100
     Both this, th'Hesperian garden, Cadmus' story,
     Jove's shower, the boon of Midas, Argus' eyes,
     Boccace his Demogorgon, thousands more,
     All abstract riddles of our stone. How now?

SCENE II

[Enter] FACE.

[Mam.] Do we succeed? Is our day come? And holds it?

Face. The evening will set red upon you, sir;
     You have colour for it, crimson: the red ferment
     Has done his office. Three hours hence, prepare you
     To see projection.

Mam.   Pertinax, my Surly,
     Again I say to thee aloud, 'Be rich'.
     This day thou shalt have ingots, and tomorrow
     Give lords th'affront. Is it, my Zephyrus, right?
     Blushes the bolt's head?

Face.   Like a wench with child, sir,
That were but now discovered to her master.   10
Mam. Excellent witty Lungs! My only care is
Where to get stuff enough now to project on:
This town will not half serve me.
Face.   No, sir? Buy
The covering off o' churches.
Mam.   That's true.
Face.   Yes.
Let 'em stand bare, as do their auditory.
Or cap 'em new with shingles.
Mam.   No, good thatch:
Thatch will lie light upo' the rafters, Lungs.
Lungs, I will manumit thee from the furnace;
I will restore thee thy complexion, Puff,
Lost in the embers; and repair this brain   20
Hurt wi' the fume o' the metals.
Face.   I have blown, sir,
Hard for your worship; thrown by many a coal
When 'twas not beech; weighed those I put in, just,
To keep your heat still even; these bleared eyes
Have waked to read your several colours, sir,
Of the pale citron, the green lion, the crow,
The peacock's tail, the plumed swan.
Mam.   And lastly,
Thou hast descried the flower, the *sanguis agni*?
Face. Yes, sir.
Mam.   Where's master?
Face.   At's prayers, sir: he,
Good man, he's doing his devotions   30
For the success.
Mam.   Lungs, I will set a period
To all thy labours: thou shalt be the master
Of my seraglio.
Face.   Good, sir.
Mam.   But do you hear?
I'll geld you, Lungs.
Face.   Yes, sir.

Mam.   For I do mean
   To have a list of wives and concubines
   Equal with Solomon, who had the stone
   Alike with me; and I will make me a back
   With the elixir that shall be as tough
   As Hercules, to encounter fifty a night.
   Th'art sure, thou saw'st it blood?
Face.   Both blood and spirit,
   sir.   40
Mam. I will have all my beds blown up, not stuffed:
   Down is too hard. And then, mine oval room
   Filled with such pictures as Tiberius took
   From Elephantis, and dull Aretine
   But coldly imitated. Then, my glasses
   Cut in more subtle angles, to disperse
   And multiply the figures, as I walk
   Naked between my *succubae*. My mists
   I'll have of perfume, vapoured 'bout the room
   To lose ourselves in; and my baths like pits   50
   To fall into; from whence we will come forth
   And roll us dry in gossamer and roses.
   (Is it arrived at ruby?) – Where I spy
   A wealthy citizen or rich lawyer
   Have a sublimed pure wife, unto that fellow
   I'll send a thousand pound to be my cuckold.
Face. And I shall carry it?
Mam.   No. I'll ha' no bawds
   But fathers and mothers. They will do it best,
   Best of all others. And my flatterers
   Shall be the pure and gravest of divines   60
   That I can get for money. My mere fools,
   Eloquent burgesses; and then my poets,
   The same that writ so subtly of the fart,
   Whom I will entertain still for that subject.
   The few that would give out themselves to be
   Court and town stallions, and each-where belie
   Ladies who are known most innocent for them,

Those will I beg to make me eunuchs of,
And they shall fan me with ten ostrich tails
Apiece, made in a plume to gather wind.   70
We will be brave, Puff, now we ha' the med'cine.
My meat shall all come in in Indian shells,
Dishes of agate set in gold and studded
With emeralds, sapphires, hyacinths and rubies:
The tongues of carps, dormice, and camels' heels,
Boiled i' the spirit of *Sol*, and dissolved pearl
(Apicius' diet, 'gainst the epilepsy);
And I will eat these broths with spoons of amber,
Headed with diamond and carbuncle.
My foot-boy shall eat pheasants, calvered salmons,   80
Knots, godwits, lampreys; I myself will have
The beards of barbels served instead of salads;
Oiled mushrooms; and the swelling unctuous paps
Of a fat pregnant sow, newly cut off,
Dressed with an exquisite and poignant sauce;
For which I'll say unto my cook, 'There's gold;
Go forth, and be a knight'.

Face.   Sir, I'll go look
A little, how it heightens.

Mam.   Do.   [*Exit Face*.]
                         My shirts
I'll have of taffeta-sarsnet, soft and light
As cobwebs; and for all my other raiment,   90
It shall be such as might provoke the Persian,
Were he to teach the world riot anew.
My gloves of fishes' and birds' skins, perfumed
With gums of paradise, and eastern air —

Sur. And do you think to have the stone, with this?

Mam. No, I do think t'have all this, with the stone.

Sur. Why, I have heard he must be *homo frugi*,
A pious, holy and religious man,
One free from mortal sin, a very virgin.

Mam. That makes it, sir, he is so. But I buy it.   100
My venture brings it me. He, honest wretch,

A notable, superstitious, good soul,
Has worn his knees bare and his slippers bald
With prayer and fasting for it; and, sir, let him
Do it alone for me, still. Here he comes:
Not a profane word afore him; 'tis poison.

SCENE III

[*Enter*] SUBTLE.

[*Mam.*] Good morrow, Father.
Sub.   Gentle son, good morrow.
    And your friend, there. What is he, is with you?
Mam. An heretic that I did bring along
    In hope, sir, to convert him.
Sub.   Son, I doubt
    You're covetous, that thus you meet your time
    I' the just point; prevent your day at morning.
    This argues something worthy of a fear
    Of importune and carnal appetite.
    Take heed you do not cause the blessing leave you
    With your ungoverned haste. I should be sorry   10
    To see my labours, now e'en at perfection,
    Got by long watching and large patience,
    Not prosper where my love and zeal hath placed 'em.
    Which (heaven I call to witness, with yourself,
    To whom I have poured my thoughts) in all my ends,
    Have looked no way but unto public good,
    To pious uses, and dear charity,
    Now grown a prodigy with men. Wherein
    If you, my son, should now prevaricate,
    And to your own particular lusts employ   20
    So great and catholic a bliss, be sure
    A curse will follow, yea, and overtake
    Your subtle and most secret ways.
Mam.   I know, sir,

SC. III]   THE ALCHEMIST   57

> You shall not need to fear me. I but come
> To ha' you confute this gentleman.

Sur.   Who is,
> Indeed, sir, somewhat costive of belief
> Toward your stone: would not be gulled.

Sub.   Well, son,
> All that I can convince him in, is this:
> The work is done; bright *Sol* is in his robe.
> We have a med'cine of the triple soul,   30
> The glorified spirit. Thanks to be heaven,
> And make us worthy of it. Ulenspiegel!

[*Enter* FACE.]

Face. Anon, sir.

Sub.   Look well to the register,
> And let your heat still lessen by degrees,
> To the aludels.

Face.   Yes, sir.

Sub.   Did you look
> O' the bolt's head yet?

Face.   Which? On D, sir?

Sub.   Ay.
> What's the complexion?

Face.   Whitish.

Sub.   Infuse vinegar
> To draw his volatile substance and his tincture,
> And let the water in glass E be filtered,
> And put into the gripe's egg. Lute him well,   40
> And leave him closed in *balneo*.

Face.   I will, sir.   [*Exit.*]

Sur. What a brave language here is, next to canting!

Sub. I have another work you never saw, son,
> That, three days since, passed the philosopher's wheel,
> In the lent heat of athanor, and's become
> Sulphor o' nature.

Mam.   But 'tis for me?

Sub.   What need you?

You have enough in that is perfect.

Mam.   O, but –

Sub. Why, this is covetise!

Mam.   No, I assure you,
I shall employ it all in pious uses,
Founding of colleges and grammar schools,   50
Marrying young virgins, building hospitals
And, now and then, a church.

[Enter FACE.*]*

Sub.   How now?

Face.   Sir, please you,
Shall I not change the filter?

Sub.   Marry, yes.
And bring me the complexion of glass B.   *[Exit Face.]*

Mam. Ha' you another?

Sub.   Yes, son; were I assured
Your piety were firm, we would not want
The means to glorify it. But I hope the best.
I mean to tinct C in sand-heat tomorrow,
And give him imbibition.

Mam.   Of white oil?

Sub. No, sir, of red. F is come over the helm too,   60
I thank my Maker, in St Mary's bath,
And shows *lac virginis.* Blessed be heaven.
I sent you of his faeces there, calcined.
Out of that calx I ha' won the salt of mercury.

Mam. By pouring on your rectified water?

Sub. Yes, and reverberating in athanor.

[Enter FACE.*]*

How now? What colour says it?

Face.   The ground black, sir.

Mam. That's your crow's head?

Sur.   Your coxcomb's, is't not?

Sub. No, 'tis not perfect. Would it were the crow.
That work wants something.

Sur. [*Aside*]　　　　　　　　O, I looked for this.　　70
　　The hay is a-pitching.
Sub.　　　　　　　　　Are you sure you loosed 'em
　　I' their own menstrue?
Face.　　　　　　　　　Yes, sir, and then married 'em,
　　And put 'em in a bolt's-head, nipped to digestion,
　　According as you bade me when I set
　　The liquor of Mars to circulation
　　In the same heat.
Sub.　　　　　　　　The process, then, was right.
Face. Yes, by the token, sir, the retort brake,
　　And what was saved was put into the pelican,
　　And signed with Hermes' seal.
Sub.　　　　　　　　　　I think 'twas so.
　　We should have a new *amalgama*.
Sur. [*Aside*]　　　　　　　O, this ferret　　80
　　Is rank as any polecat.
Sub.　　　　　　　But I care not.
　　Let him e'en die; we have enough beside
　　In *embrion*. H has his white shirt on?
Face.　　　　　　　　　　Yes, sir,
　　He's ripe for inceration: he stands warm
　　In his ash-fire. I would not you should let
　　Any die now, if I might counsel, sir,
　　For luck's sake to the rest. It is not good.
Mam. He says right.
Sur. [*Aside*]　　　Ay, are you bolted?
Face.　　　　　　　　　Nay, I know't, sir;
　　I have seen th'ill fortune. What is some three ounces
　　Of fresh materials?
Mam.　　　　　　Is't no more?
Face.　　　　　　　　　No more, sir,　　90
　　Of gold t'amalgam with some six of mercury.
Mam. Away, here's money. What will serve?
Face.　　　　　　　　　Ask him, sir.
Mam. How much?
Sub.　　　　Give him nine pound; you may gi' him ten.

Sur. [*Aside*] Yes, twenty, and be cozened; do.
Mam.   There 'tis.
Sub. This needs not, but that you will have it so
    To see conclusions of all. For two
    Of our inferior works are at fixation.
    A third is in ascension. Go your ways.
    Ha' you set the oil of *Luna* in Kemia?
Face. Yes, sir.
Sub.   And the philosopher's vinegar?
Face.   Ay. [*Exit.*]   100
Sur. [*Aside*] We shall have a salad.
Mam.   When do you make
    projection?
Sub. Son, be not hasty. I exalt our med'cine
    By hanging him in *balneo vaporoso*,
    And giving him solution; then congeal him;
    And then dissolve him; then again congeal him:
    For look, how oft I iterate the work,
    So many times I add unto his virtue.
    As, if at first one ounce convert a hundred,
    After his second loose, he'll turn a thousand;
    His third solution, ten; his fourth, a hundred;   110
    After his fifth, a thousand thousand ounces
    Of any imperfect metal, into pure
    Silver or gold, in all examinations
    As good as any of the natural mine.
    Get you your stuff here against afternoon:
    Your brass, your pewter, and your andirons.
Mam. Not those of iron?
Sub.   Yes, you may bring them, too.
    We'll change all metals.
Sur. [*Aside*]   I believe you in that.
Mam. Then I may send my spits?
Sub.   Yes, and your racks.
Sur. And dripping-pans, and pot-hangers, and hooks,   120
    Shall he not?
Sub.   If he please.

Sur.   To be an ass.

Sub. How, sir!

Mam.   This gent'man you must bear withal.
    I told you he had no faith.

Sur.   And little hope, sir,
    But much less charity, should I gull myself.

Sub. Why, what have you observed, sir, in our art
    Seems so impossible?

Sur.   But your whole work, no more.
    That you should hatch gold in a furnace, sir,
    As they do eggs in Egypt!

Sub.   Sir, do you
    Believe that eggs are hatched so?

Sur.   If I should?

Sub. Why, I think that the greater miracle.   130
    No egg but differs from a chicken more
    Than metals in themselves.

Sur.   That cannot be.
    The egg's ordained by nature to that end,
    And is a chicken in *potentia*.

Sub. The same we say of lead and other metals,
    Which would be gold, if they had time.

Mam.   And that
    Our art doth further.

Sub.   Ay, for 'twere absurd
    To think that nature in the earth bred gold
    Perfect, i' the instant. Something went before.
    There must be remote matter.

Sur.   Ay, what is that?   140

Sub. Marry, we say —

Mam.   Ay, now it heats: stand, Father,
    Pound him to dust —

Sub.   It is, of the one part,
    A humid exhalation, which we call
    Materia liquida, or the unctuous water;
    On th'other part, a certain crass and viscous
    Portion of earth; both which, concorporate,

Do make the elementary matter of gold:
Which is not yet *propria materia*,
But common to all metals and all stones.
For where it is forsaken of that moisture,   150
And hath more dryness, it becomes a stone;
Where it retains more of the humid fatness,
It turns to sulphur or to quicksilver,
Who are the parents of all other metals.
Nor can this remote matter suddenly
Progress so from extreme unto extreme,
As to grow gold, and leap o'er all the means.
Nature doth first beget th'imperfect, then
Proceeds she to the perfect. Of that airy
And oily water, mercury is engendered;   160
Sulphur o' the fat and earthy part: the one
(Which is the last) supplying the place of male,
The other of the female, in all metals.
Some do believe hermaphrodeity,
That both do act and suffer. But these two
Make the rest ductile, malleable, extensive.
And even in gold they are; for we do find
Seeds of them by our fire, and gold in them;
And can produce the species of each metal
More perfect thence than nature doth in earth.   170
Beside, who doth not see in daily practice
Art can beget bees, hornets, beetles, wasps,
Out of the carcasses and dung of creatures;
Yea, scorpions of an herb, being ritely placed:
And these are living creatures, far more perfect
And excellent than metals.

Mam.   Well said, Father!
Nay, if he take you in hand, sir, with an argument,
He'll bray you in a mortar.

Sur.   'Pray you, sir, stay.
Rather than I'll be brayed, sir, I'll believe
That alchemy is a pretty kind of game,   180
Somewhat like tricks o' the cards, to cheat a man
With charming.

Sub.   Sir?

Sur.   What else are all your terms,
    Whereon no one o' your writers 'grees with other?
    Of your elixir, your *lac virginis*,
    Your stone, your med'cine, and your chrysosperm,
    Your *sal*, your sulphur, and your mercury,
    Your oil of height, your tree of life, your blood,
    Your marcasite, your tutty, your magnesia,
    Your toad, your crow, your dragon, and your panther,
    Your sun, your moon, your firmament, your adrop, 190
    Your lato, azoch, zernich, chibrit, heautarit,
    And then your red man, and your white woman,
    With all your broths, your menstrues, and materials
    Of piss, and egg-shells, women's terms, man's blood,
    Hair o' the head, burnt clouts, chalk, merds, and clay,
    Powder of bones, scalings of iron, glass,
    And worlds of other strange ingredients,
    Would burst a man to name?

Sub.   And all these, named,
    Intending but one thing: which art our writers
    Used to obscure their art.

Mam.   Sir, so I told him,   200
    Because the simple idiot should not learn it,
    And make it vulgar.

Sub.   Was not all the knowledge
    Of the Egyptians writ in mystic symbols?
    Speak not the Scriptures oft in parables?
    Are not the choicest fables of the poets,
    That were the fountains and first springs of wisdom,
    Wrapped in perplexèd allegories?

Mam.   I urged that,
    And cleared to him that Sisyphus was damned
    To roll the ceaseless stone only because
    He would have made ours common.

DOLL is seen.

                       Who is this?   210
Sub. God's precious – what do you mean? Go in, good lady,

Let me entreat you.   [*Exit Doll.*]

          Where's this varlet?

[*Enter* FACE.]

Face.   Sir?

Sub. You very knave! Do you use me thus?

Face.   Wherein, sir?

Sub. Go in and see, you traitor. Go!   [*Exit Face.*]

Mam.   Who is it, sir?

Sub. Nothing, sir. Nothing.

Mam.   What's the matter? Good sir!

    I have not seen you thus distempered. Who is't?

Sub. All arts have still had, sir, their adversaries,

    But ours the most ignorant –

FACE *returns.*

                  What now?

Face. 'Twas not my fault, sir. She would speak with you.

Sub. Would she, sir? Follow me.   [*Exit.*]

Mam.   Stay, Lungs.

Face.   I dare not, sir. 220

Mam. How! 'Pray thee, stay.

Face.   She's mad, sir, and sent hither –

Mam. Stay man, what is she?

Face.   A lord's sister, sir.

    (He'll be mad too –

Mam.   I warrant thee.) Why sent hither?

Face. Sir, to be cured.

Sub. [*Within*]   Why, rascal!

Face.   Lo, you. Here, sir!

                           He goes out.

Mam. 'Fore-God, a Bradamante, a brave piece.

Sur. 'Heart, this is a bawdy-house! I'll be burnt else.

Mam. O, by this light, no! Do not wrong him. He's

    Too scrupulous that way. It is his vice.

    No, he's a rare physician, do him right;

    An excellent Paracelsian! And has done   230

Strange cures with mineral physic. He deals all
With spirits, he. He will not hear a word
Of Galen, or his tedious recipes.

[*Enter*] FACE *again*.

How, now, Lungs!
Face.   Softly, sir, speak softly. I meant
To ha' told your worship all. This must not hear.
Mam. No, he will not be gulled; let him alone.
Face. You're very right. Sir, she is a most rare scholar,
And is gone mad with studying Broughton's works.
If you but name a word touching the Hebrew,
She falls into her fit, and will discourse   240
So learnedly of genealogies
As you would run mad, too, to hear, sir.
Mam. How might one do t'have conference with her, Lungs?
Face. O, divers have run mad upon the conference.
I do not know, sir: I am sent in haste
To fetch a vial.
Sur.   Be not gulled, Sir Mammon.
Mam. Wherein? 'Pray ye, be patient.
Sur.   Yes, as you are;
And trust confederate knaves, and bawds, and whores.
Mam. You are too foul, believe it. Come here, Ulen,
One word.
Face.   I dare not, in good faith.
Mam.   Stay, knave.   250
Face. He's extreme angry that you saw her, sir.
Mam. Drink that. [*Giving him money*] What is she, when she's
out of her fit?
Face. O, the most affablest creature, sir! So merry!
So pleasant! She'll mount you up like quicksilver
Over the helm, and circulate like oil,
A very vegetal; discourse of state,
Of mathematics, bawdry, anything —
Mam. Is she no way accessible? No means,
No trick, to give a man a taste of her — wit —

          Or so?

[*Sub.* (*Within*)] Ulen!

Face.   I'll come to you again, sir.   [*Exit.*]   260

Mam. Surly, I did not think one o' your breeding
          Would traduce personages of worth.

Sur.   Sir Epicure,
          Your friend to use, yet still loath to be gulled.
          I do not like your philosophical bawds.
          Their stone is lechery enough to pay for,
          Without this bait.

Mam.   'Heart, you abuse yourself.
          I know the lady, and her friends, and means,
          The original of this disaster. Her brother
          Has told me all.

Sur.   And yet you ne'er saw her
          Till now?

Mam.   O, yes, but I forgot. I have (believe it)   270
          One o' the treacherous'st memories, I do think,
          Of all mankind.

Sur.   What call you her – brother?

Mam.   My lord –
          He wi' not have his name known, now I think on't.

Sur. A very treacherous memory!

Mam.   O' my faith –

Sur. Tut, if you ha' it not about you, pass it
          Till we meet next.

Mam.   Nay, by this hand, 'tis true.
          He's one I honour, and my noble friend,
          And I respect his house.

Sur.   'Heart! Can it be
          That a grave sir, a rich, that has no need,
          A wise sir, too, at other times, should thus   280
          With his own oaths and arguments make hard means
          To gull himself? And this be your elixir,
          Your *lapis mineralis*, and your lunary,
          Give me your honest trick yet at primero
          Or gleek; and take your *lutum sapientis*,

Your *menstruum simplex*: I'll have gold before you,
And with less danger of the quicksilver
Or the hot sulphur!

[*Enter* FACE.]

Face. (*To Surly*)
                    Here's one from Captain Face, sir,
Desires you meet him i' the Temple church,
Some half-hour hence, and upon earnest business.   290
(*He whispers [to] Mammon.*) Sir, if you please to quit
  us now, and come
Again within two hours, you shall have
My master busy examining o' the works;
And I will steal you in unto the party,
That you may see her converse. [*To Surly*] Sir, shall I say
You'll meet the Captain's worship?
Sur.   Sir, I will.
[*Aside*] But by attorney, and to a second purpose.
Now I am sure it is a bawdy-house;
I'll swear it, were the marshal here to thank me:
The naming this commander doth confirm it.   300
Don Face! Why he's the most authentic dealer
I' these commodities! The superintendent
To all the quainter traffickers in town.
He is their visitor, and does appoint
Who lies with whom, and at what hour, what price,
Which gown; and in what smock, what fall, what tire.
Him will I prove, by a third person, to find
The subtleties of this dark labyrinth;
Which, if I do discover, dear Sir Mammon,
You'll give your poor friend leave, though no
  philosopher,   310
To laugh; for you that are, 'tis thought, shall weep.
Face. Sir. He does pray you'll not forget.
Sur.   I will not, sir.
Sir Epicure, I shall leave you?
Mam.   I follow you, straight.

                                               [*Exit Surly.*]

Face. But do so, good sir, to avoid suspicion.
   This gent'man has a parlous head.
Mam.   But wilt thou, Ulen,
   Be constant to thy promise?
Face.   As my life, sir.
Mam. And wilt thou insinuate what I am? And praise me?
   And say I am a noble fellow?
Face.   O, what else, sir?
   And that you'll make her royal with the stone,
   An empress; and yourself king of Bantam.   320
Mam. Wilt thou do this?
Face.   Will I, sir?
Mam.   Lungs, my Lungs!
   I love thee.
Face.   Send your stuff, sir, that my master
   May busy himself about projection.
Mam. Th'hast witched me, rogue: [*Giving him money*] take, go.
Face.   Your jack and all, sir.
Mam. Thou art a villain – I will send my jack,
   And the weights too. Slave, I could bite thine ear.
   Away, thou dost not care for me.
Face.   Not I, sir?
Mam. Come, I was born to make thee, my good weasel;
   Set thee on a bench, and ha' thee twirl a chain
   With the best lords' vermin of 'em all.
Face.   Away, sir.   330
Mam. A Count, nay, a Count Palatine –
Face.   Good sir, go.
Mam. Shall not advance thee better: no, nor faster.   [*Exit.*]

SCENE IV

[*Enter*] SUBTLE [*and*] DOLL.

[*Sub.*] Has he bit? Has he bit?

Face.   And swallowed too, my Subtle.
    I ha' giv'n him line, and now he plays, i' faith.
Sub. And shall we twitch him?
Face.   Thorough both the gills.
    A wench is a rare bait, with which a man
    No sooner's taken, but he straight firks mad.
Sub. Doll, my lord What's'hum's sister, you must now
    Bear yourself *statelich.*
Doll.   O, let me alone.
    I'll not forget my race, I warrant you.
    I'll keep my distance, laugh, and talk aloud;
    Have all the tricks of a proud scurvy lady,   10
    And be as rude as her woman.
Face.   Well said, Sanguine.
Sub. But will he send his andirons?
Face.   His jack too,
    And's iron shoeing-horn: I ha' spoke to him. Well,
    I must not lose my wary gamester, yonder.
Sub. O, Monsieur Caution, that will not be gulled?
Face.   Ay,
    If I can strike a fine hook into him now –
    The Temple church, there I have cast mine angle.
    Well, pray for me. I'll about it.   *One knocks.*
Sub.   What, more gudgeons!
    Doll, scout, scout! Stay, Face, you must go to the door.
    'Pray God it be my Anabaptist. Who is't, Doll?   20
Doll. I know him not. He looks like a gold-end man.
Sub. Gods so! 'Tis he, he said he would send. What call you
        him?
    The sanctified elder, that should deal
    For Mammon's jack and andirons! Let him in.
    Stay, help me off first with my gown.   [*Exit Face.*]
                                        Away,
    Madam, to your withdrawing chamber.   [*Exit Doll.*]
                                        Now,
    In a new tune, new gesture, but old language.
    This fellow is sent from one negotiates with me

About the stone, too, for the holy brethren
Of Amsterdam, the exiled saints that hope   30
To raise their discipline by it. I must use him
In some strange fashion now, to make him admire me.

SCENE V

[*Enter*] ANANIAS.

[*Sub.*] Where is my drudge?

[*Enter* FACE.]

Face.   Sir.
Sub.   Take away the recipient,
  And rectify your menstrue from the *phlegma*.
  Then pour it o' the *Sol* in the cucurbite,
  And let 'em macerate together.
Face.   Yes, sir.
  And save the ground?
Sub.   No. *Terra damnata*
  Must not have entrance in the work. [*To Ananias*]
    Who are you?
Ana. A faithful brother, if it please you.
Sub.   What's that?
  A Lullianist? A Ripley? *Filius artis*?
  Can you sublime and dulcify? Calcine?
  Know you the *sapor pontic*? *Sapor styptic*?   10
  Or what is homogene or heterogene?
Ana. I understand no heathen language, truly.
Sub. Heathen, you Knipper-Doling? Is *Ars sacra*,
  Or chrysopoeia, or spagyrica,
  Of the pamphysic, or panarchic knowledge,
  A heathen language?
Ana.   Heathen Greek, I take it.
Sub. How? Heathen Greek?
Ana.   All's heathen, but the Hebrew.

Sub. Sirrah, my varlet, stand you forth, and speak to him
         Like a philosopher: answer i' the language.
         Name the vexations and the martyrizations   20
         Of metals in the work.
Face.   Sir, putrefaction,
         Solution, ablution, sublimation,
         Cohobation, calcination, ceration, and
         Fixation.
Sub.   This is heathen Greek to you, now?
         And when comes vivification?
Face.   After mortification.
Sub. What's cohobation?
Face.   'Tis the pouring on
         Your *aqua regis*, and then drawing him off
         To the trine circle of the seven spheres.
Sub. What's the proper passion of metals?
Face.   Malleation.
Sub. What's your *ultimum supplicium auri*?
Face.   Antimonium.   30
Sub. This's heathen Greek to you? And what's your mercury?
Face. A very fugitive: he will be gone, sir.
Sub. How know you him?
Face.   By his viscosity,
         His oleosity, and his suscitability.
Sub. How do you sublime him?
Face.   With the calce of eggshells,
         White marble, talc.
Sub.   Your *magisterium,* now?
         What's that?
Face.   Shifting, sir, your elements,
         Dry into cold, cold into moist, moist in-
         To hot, hot into dry.
Sub.   This's heathen Greek to you still?
         Your *lapis philosophicus*?
Face.   'Tis a stone, and not   40
         A stone; a spirit, a soul, and a body;
         Which if you do dissolve, it is dissolved,

   If you coagulate, it is coagulated,
   If you make it to fly, it flieth.
Sub.   Enough.   [*Exit Face.*]
   This's heathen Greek to you? What are you, sir?
Ana. Please you, a servant of the exiled brethren,
   That deal with widows' and with orphans' goods,
   And make a just account unto the saints:
   A deacon.
Sub.   O, you are sent from Master Wholesome,
   Your teacher?
Ana.   From Tribulation Wholesome,   50
   Our very zealous pastor.
Sub.   Good. I have
   Some orphans' goods to come here.
Ana.   Of what kind, sir?
Sub. Pewter and brass, andirons and kitchen ware,
   Metals that we must use our med'cine on;
   Wherein the brethren may have a penn'orth,
   For ready money.
Ana.   Were the orphans' parents
   Sincere professors?
Sub.   Why do you ask?
Ana.   Because
   We then are to deal justly, and give in truth
   Their utmost value.
Sub.   'Slid, you'd cozen else,
   And if their parents were not of the faithful?   60
   I will not trust you, now I think on't,
   Till I ha' talked with your pastor. Ha' you brought money
   To buy more coals?
Ana.   No, surely.
Sub.   No? How so?
Ana. The brethren bid me say unto you, sir,
   Surely they will not venture any more
   Till they may see projection.
Sub.   How!
Ana.   You've had

For the instruments, as bricks, and loam, and glasses,
Already thirty pound; and for materials,
They say, some ninety more; and they have heard, since,
That one at Heidelberg made it of an egg   70
And a small paper of pin-dust.
Sub.   What's your name?
Ana. My name is Ananias.
Sub.   Out, the varlet
That cozened the Apostles! Hence, away,
Flee, Mischief! Had your holy consistory
No name to send me of another sound
Than wicked Ananias? Send your elders
Hither to make atonement for you quickly,
And gi' me satisfaction; or out goes
The fire, and down th'alembics and the furnace,
Piger Henricus, or what not. Thou wretch,   80
Both *sericon* and *bufo* shall be lost,
Tell 'em. All hope of rooting out the bishops
Or th'antichristian hierarchy shall perish,
If they stay threescore minutes. The aqueity,
Terreity, and sulphureity
Shall run together again, and all be annulled,
Thou wicked Ananias.   [*Exit Ananias.*]
                    This will fetch 'em,
And make 'em haste towards their gulling more.
A man must deal like a rough nurse, and fright
Those that are froward to an appetite.   90

SCENE VI

[*Enter*] FACE [*and*] DRUGGER.

[*Face.*] He's busy with his spirits, but we'll upon him.
Sub. How now! What mates? What Bayards ha' we here?
Face. I told you he would be furious. Sir, here's Nab
Has brought y'another piece of gold to look on –

[*To Drugger*] We must appease him. Give it me – and prays
      you,
  You would devise – what is it, Nab?
Dru.   A sign, sir.
Face. Ay, a good lucky one, a thriving sign, Doctor.
Sub. I was devising now.
Face. [*Aside to Subtle*]   'Slight, do not say so,
  He will repent he ga' you any more. –
  What say you to his constellation, Doctor?   10
  The balance?
Sub.   No, that way is stale and common.
  A townsman, born in Taurus, gives the bull,
  Or the bull's head; in Aries, the ram:
  A poor device. No, I will have his name
  Formed in some mystic character, whose *radii*,
  Striking the senses of the passers-by,
  Shall, by a virtual influence, breed affections
  That may result upon the party owns it:
  As thus –
Face.   Nab!
Sub.   He first shall have a bell, that's Abel;
  And by it, standing one whose name is Dee,   20
  In a rug gown; there's D and Rug, that's Drug;
  And right anenst him, a dog snarling, 'er':
  There's Drugger, Abel Drugger. That's his sign.
  And here's now mystery and hieroglyphic!
Face. Abel, thou art made.
Dru.   Sir, I do thank his worship.
Face. Six o' thy legs more will not do it, Nab.
  He has brought you a pipe of tobacco, Doctor.
Dru.   Yes, sir.
  I have another thing I would impart –
Face. Out with it, Nab.
Dru.   Sir, there is lodged, hard by me,
  A rich young widow –
Face.   Good! A *bona roba*?   30
Dru. But nineteen, at the most.

Face.　　　　　　　　　　Very good, Abel.

Dru. Marry, she's not in fashion yet: she wears
　　A hood, but't stands a-cop.

Face.　　　　　　　　　　No matter, Abel.

Dru. And I do now and then give her a fucus –

Face. What! Dost thou deal, Nab?

Sub.　　　　　　　　　I did tell you, Captain.

Dru. And physic too, sometime, sir, for which she trusts me
　　With all her mind. She's come up here of purpose
　　To learn the fashion.

Face.　　　　　　　Good. [*Aside*] His match too!
　　– On, Nab.

Dru. And she does strangely long to know her fortune.

Face. God's lid, Nab, send her to the Doctor, hither.　　40

Dru. Yes, I have spoke to her of his worship already,
　　But she's afraid it will be blown abroad,
　　And hurt her marriage.

Face.　　　　　　　　Hurt it? 'Tis the way
　　To heal it, if 'twere hurt; to make it more
　　Followed and sought. Nab, thou shalt tell her this.
　　She'll be more known, more talked of, and your widows
　　Are ne'er of any price till they be famous:
　　Their honour is their multitude of suitors.
　　Send her, it may be thy good fortune. What?
　　Thou dost not know?

Dru.　　　　　　　　No, sir, she'll never marry　　50
　　Under a knight. Her brother has made a vow.

Face. What, and dost thou despair, my little Nab,
　　Knowing what the Doctor has set down for thee,
　　And seeing so many o' the city dubbed?
　　One glass o' thy water, with a madam I know,
　　Will have it done, Nab. What's her brother? A knight?

Dru. No, sir, a gentleman newly warm in his land, sir,
　　Scarce cold in his one and twenty; that does govern
　　His sister here, and is a man himself
　　Of some three thousand a year, and is come up　　60
　　To learn to quarrel and to live by his wits,

And will go down again and die i' the country.
Face. How! To quarrel?
Dru.   Yes, sir, to carry quarrels
  As gallants do, and manage 'em by line.
Face. 'Slid, Nab! The Doctor is the only man
  In Christendom for him. He has made a table,
  With mathematical demonstrations,
  Touching the art of quarrels. He will give him
  An instrument to quarrel by. Go, bring 'em both,
  Him and his sister. And, for thee, with her   70
  The Doctor happ'ly may persuade. Go to.
  'Shalt give his worship a new damask suit
  Upon the premises.
Sub.   O, good Captain!
Face.   He shall:
  He is the honestest fellow, Doctor. Stay not;
  No offers; bring the damask, and the parties.
Dru. I'll try my power, sir.
Face.   And thy will too, Nab.
Sub. 'Tis good tobacco this! What is't an ounce?
Face. He'll send you a pound, Doctor.
Sub.   O, no!
Face.   He will do't.
  It is the goodest soul. Abel, about it;
  Thou shalt know more anon. Away, be gone.   80
                              [*Exit Drugger.*]
  A miserable rogue, and lives with cheese,
  And has the worms. That was the cause, indeed,
  Why he came now. He dealt with me in private
  To get a med'cine for 'em.
Sub.   And shall, sir. This works.
Face. A wife, a wife for one on us, my dear Subtle!
  We'll e'en draw lots, and he that fails shall have
  The more in goods, the other has in tail.
Sub. Rather the less. For she may be so light,
  She may want grains.
Face.   Ay, or be such a burden,

A man would scarce endure her for the whole.   90
Sub. Faith, best let's see her first, and then determine.
Face. Content. But Doll must ha' no breath on't.
Sub.   Mum.
    Away, you, to your Surly yonder; catch him.
Face. 'Pray God I ha' not stayed too long.
Sub.   I fear it.   [*Exeunt.*]

ACT III

SCENE I

[*Enter*] TRIBULATION [*and*] ANANIAS.

[*Tri.*] These chastisements are common to the saints,
    And such rebukes we of the separation
    Must bear with willing shoulders, as the trials
    Sent forth to tempt our frailties.
Ana.   In pure zeal,
    I do not like the man: he is a heathen,
    And speaks the language of Canaan, truly.
Tri. I think him a profane person, indeed.
Ana.   He bears
    The visible mark of the Beast in his forehead.
    And for his stone, it is a work of darkness,
    And with philosophy blinds the eye of man.   10
Tri. Good brother, we must bend unto all means
    That may give furtherance to the holy cause.
Ana. Which his cannot: the sanctified cause
    Should have a sanctified course.
Tri.   Not always necessary.
    The children of perdition are oft-times
    Made instruments even of the greatest works.
    Beside, we should give somewhat to man's nature,
    The place he lives in, still about the fire
    And fume of metals, that intoxicate
    The brain of man and make him prone to passion.   20
    Where have you greater atheists than your cooks?
    Or more profane or choleric than your glass-men?
    More antichristian than your bell-founders?

What makes the Devil so devilish, I would ask you,
– Satan, our common enemy – but his being
Perpetually about the fire, and boiling
Brimstone and ars'nic? We must give, I say,
Unto the motives and the stirrers up
Of humours in the blood. It may be so,
When as the work is done, the stone is made,　　　　30
This heat of his may turn into a zeal,
And stand up for the beauteous discipline
Against the menstruous cloth and rag of Rome.
We must await his calling, and the coming
Of the good spirit. You did fault t'upbraid him
With the brethren's blessing of Heidelberg, weighing
What need we have to hasten on the work
For the restoring of the silenced saints,
Which ne'er will be but by the philosopher's stone.
And so a learned elder, one of Scotland,　　　　40
Assured me; *aurum potabile* being
The only med'cine for the civil magistrate,
T'incline him to a feeling of the cause;
And must be daily used in the disease.
Ana. I have not edified more, truly, by man,
Not since the beautiful light first shone on me;
And I am sad my zeal hath so offended.
Tri. Let us call on him, then.
Ana.　　　　　　　　　The motion's good,
And of the spirit: I will knock first. Peace be within!

SCENE II

[*Enter*] SUBTLE.

[*Sub.*] O, are you come? 'Twas time. Your threescore
　　minutes
　　Were at the last thread, you see, and down had gone
　　Furnus acediae, turris circulatorius:

      Limbec, bolt's-head, retort and pelican

      Had all been cinders. Wicked Ananias!

      Art thou returned? Nay then, it goes down yet.

Tri. Sir, be appeased, he is come to humble

      Himself in spirit, and to ask your patience

      If too much zeal hath carried him aside

      From the due path.

Sub.   Why, this doth qualify!   10

Tri. The brethren had no purpose, verily,

      To give you the least grievance, but are ready

      To lend their willing hands to any project

      The spirit and you direct.

Sub.   This qualifies more!

Tri. And for the orphans' goods, let them be valued,

      Or what is needful else to the holy work,

      It shall be numbered; here, by me, the saints

      Throw down their purse before you.

Sub.   This qualifies most!

      Why, thus it should be: now you understand.

      Have I discoursed so unto you of our stone?   20

      And of the good that it shall bring your cause?

      Showed you (beside the main of hiring forces

      Abroad, drawing the Hollanders, your friends,

      From th'Indies to serve you with all their fleet)

      That even the med'cinal use shall make you a faction

      And party in the realm? As, put the case

      That some great man in state, he have the gout;

      Why, you but send three drops of your elixir,

      You help him straight: there you have made a friend.

      Another has the palsy or the dropsy,   30

      He takes of your incombustible stuff,

      He's young again: there you have made a friend.

      A lady that is past the feat of body,

      Though not of mind, and hath her face decayed

      Beyond all cure of paintings, you restore

      With the oil of talc: there you have made a friend,

      And all her friends. A lord that is a leper,

A knight that has the bone-ache, or a squire
That hath both these, you make 'em smooth and sound
With a bare fricace of your med'cine: still   40
You increase your friends.

Tri.   Ay, 'tis very pregnant.

Sub. And then, the turning of this lawyer's pewter
To plate at Christmas –

Ana.   Christ-tide, I pray you.

Sub. Yet, Ananias?

Ana.   I have done.

Sub.   Or changing
His parcel gilt to massy gold: you cannot
But raise your friends. Withal, to be of power
To pay an army in the field; to buy
The King of France out of his realms, or Spain
Out of his Indies; what can you not do
Against lords spiritual or temporal   50
That shall oppone you?

Tri.   Verily, 'tis true.
We may be temporal lords ourselves, I take it.

Sub. You may be anything, and leave off to make
Long-winded exercises, or suck up
Your 'ha' and 'hum' in a tune. I not deny
But such as are not gracèd in a state
May, for their ends, be adverse in religion,
And get a tune to call the flock together;
For (to say sooth) a tune does much with women
And other phlegmatic people: it is your bell.   60

Ana. Bells are profane: a tune may be religious.

Sub. No warning with you? Then farewell, my patience!
'Slight, it shall down: I will not be thus tortured.

Tri. I pray you, sir.

Sub.   All shall perish. I have spoke it.

Tri. Let me find grace, sir, in your eyes; the man,
He stands corrected; neither did his zeal
(But as yourself) allow a tune somewhere;
Which now, being to'ard the stone, we shall not need.

Sub. No, nor your holy vizard, to win widows
    To give you legacies, or make zealous wives   70
    To rob their husbands, for the common cause;
    Nor take the start of bonds, broke but one day,
    And say they were forfeited by providence.
    Nor shall you need o'ernight to eat huge meals
    To celebrate your next day's fast the better,
    The whilst the brethren and the sisters, humbled,
    Abate the stiffness of the flesh; nor cast
    Before your hungry hearers scrupulous bones,
    As whether a Christian may hawk or hunt,
    Or whether matrons of the holy assembly   80
    May lay their hair out, or wear doublets,
    Or have that idol starch about their linen.
Ana. It is, indeed, an idol.
Tri.   Mind him not, sir.
    I do command thee, spirit (of zeal, but trouble),
    To peace within him. 'Pray you, sir, go on.
Sub. Nor shall you need to libel 'gainst the prelates,
    And shorten so your ears against the hearing
    Of the next wire-drawn grace; nor, of necessity,
    Rail against plays to please the alderman
    Whose daily custard you devour; nor lie   90
    With zealous rage till you are hoarse; not one
    Of these so singular arts; nor call yourselves
    By names of Tribulation, Persecution,
    Restraint, Long-patience, and such-like, affected
    By the whole family or wood of you
    Only for glory, and to catch the ear
    Of the disciple.
Tri.   Turly sir, they are
    Ways that the godly brethren have invented
    For propagation of the glorious cause,
    As very notable means, and whereby also   100
    Themselves grow soon and profitably famous.
Sub. O, but the stone, all's idle to it! Nothing!
    The art of angels, nature's miracle,

The divine secret, that doth fly in clouds
From east to west, and whose tradition
Is not from men, but spirits.

Ana.   I hate traditions:
I do not trust them –

Tri.   Peace.

Ana.   They are Popish, all.
I will not peace. I will not –

Tri.   Ananias!

Ana. Please the profane to grieve the godly; I may not.

Sub. Well, Ananias, thou shalt overcome.   110

Tri. It is an ignorant zeal that haunts him, sir.
But truly, else, a very faithful brother,
A botcher, and a man by revelation
That hath a competent knowledge of the truth.

Sub. Has he a competent sum there i' the bag
To buy the goods within? I am made guardian,
And must, for charity and conscience sake,
Now see the most be made for my poor orphans;
Though I desire the brethren, too, good gainers.
There they are, within. When you have viewed and
    bought 'em,   120
And ta'en the inventory of what they are,
They are ready for projection; there's no more
To do: cast on the med'cine, so much silver
As there is tin there, so much gold as brass,
I'll gi' it you in, by weight.

Tri.   But how long time,
Sir, must the saints expect, yet?

Sub.   Let me see,
How's the moon, now? Eight, nine, ten days hence
He will be silver potate; then three days
Before he citronize; some fifteen days,
The *magisterium* will be perfected.   130

Ana. About the second day of the third week
In the ninth month?

Sub.   Yes, my good Ananias.

Tri. What will the orphans' goods arise to, think you?

Sub. Some hundred marks; as much as filled three cars,
Unladed now: you'll make six millions of 'em.
But I must ha' more coals laid in.

Tri.   How!

Sub.   Another load,
And then we ha' finished. We must now increase
Our fire to *ignis ardens*; we are past
Fimus equinus, balnei, cineris,
And all those lenter heats. If the holy purse   140
Should, with this draught, fall low, and that the saints
Do need a present sum, I have a trick
To melt the pewter you shall buy now, instantly,
And with a tincture, make you as good Dutch dollars
As any are in Holland.

Tri.   Can you so?

Sub. Ay, and shall bide the third examination.

Ana. It will be joyful tidings to the brethren.

Sub. But you must carry it secret.

Tri.   Ay, but stay;
This act of coining, is it lawful?

Ana.   Lawful?
We know no magistrate; or, if we did,   150
This's foreign coin.

Sub.   It is no coining, sir.
It is but casting.

Tri.   Ha? You distinguish well.
Casting of money may be lawful.

Ana.   'Tis, sir.

Tri. Truly, I take it so.

Sub.   There is no scruple,
Sir, to be made of it; believe Ananias:
This case of conscience he is studied in.

Tri. I'll make a question of it to the brethren.

Ana. The brethren shall approve it lawful, doubt not.
Where shall't be done?

Sub.   For that we'll talk anon.

                                        Knock without.

There's some to speak with me. Go in, I pray you,   160
And view the parcels. That's the inventory.
I'll come to you straight. [*Exeunt Tribulation and Ananias.*]
                    Who is it? Face! Appear.

                    SCENE III

                    [*Enter*] FACE.

[*Sub.*] How now? Good prize?
Face.   Good pox! Yond' costive cheater
     Never came on.
Sub.   How then?
Face.   I ha' walked the round
     Till now, and no such thing.
Sub.   And ha' you quit him?
Face. Quit him? And hell would quit him too, he were happy.
     'Slight, would you have me stalk like a mill-jade,
     All day, for one that will not yield us grains?
     I know him of old.
Sub.   O, but to ha' gulled him
     Had been a mastery.
Face.   Let him go, black boy,
     And turn thee, that some fresh news may possess thee.
     A noble Count, a Don of Spain (my dear   10
     Delicious compeer, and my party-bawd)
     Who is come hither, private, for his conscience,
     And brought munition with him, six great slops,
     Bigger than three Dutch hoys, beside round trunks,
     Furnished with pistolets and pieces of eight,
     Will straight be here, my rogue, to have thy bath
     (That is the colour) and to make his batt'ry
     Upon our Doll, our castle, our Cinque Port,
     Our Dover pier, our what thou wilt. Where is she?
     She must prepare perfumes, delicate linen,   20
     The bath in chief, a banquet, and her wit;
     For she must milk his epididymis.
     Where is the doxy?

Sub.   I'll send her to thee;
     And but dispatch my brace of little John Leydens,
     And come again myself.
Face.   Are they within then?
Sub. Numb'ring the sum.
Face.   How much?
Sub.   A hundred marks, boy.
                                        [*Exit*.]
Face. Why, this's a lucky day! Ten pounds of Mammon!
     Three o' my clerk! A portague o' my grocer!
     This o' the brethren! Beside reversions
     And states to come i' the widow and my Count!   30
     My share today will not be bought for forty –

                    [*Enter* DOLL.]

Doll.   What?
Face. Pounds, dainty Dorothy. Art thou so near?
Doll. Yes. Say, Lord General, how fares our camp?
Face. As with the few that had entrenched themselves
     Safe, by their discipline, against a world, Doll,
     And laughed within those trenches, and grew fat
     With thinking on the booties, Doll, brought in
     Daily by their small parties. This dear hour
     A doughty Don is taken with my Doll,
     And thou mayst make his ransom what thou wilt,   40
     My dousabel: he shall be brought here, fettered
     With thy fair looks before he sees thee, and thrown
     In a down-bed, as dark as any dungeon;
     Where thou shalt keep him waking with thy drum –
     Thy drum, my Doll, thy drum! – till he be tame
     As the poor blackbirds were i' the great frost,
     Or bees are with a basin; and so hive him
     I' the swan-skin coverlid and cambric sheets,
     Till he work honey and wax, my little God's gift.
Doll. What is he, General?
Face.   An *adalantado*,   50
     A grandee, girl. Was not my Dapper here yet?

Doll. No.
Face.   Nor my Drugger?
Doll.   Neither.
Face.   A pox on 'em,
They are so long a-furnishing! Such stinkards
Would not be seen upon these festival days.

[*Enter* SUBTLE.]

How now! Ha' you done?
Sub.   Done. They are gone. The sum
Is here in bank, my Face. I would we knew
Another chapman now would buy 'em outright.
Face. 'Slid, Nab shall do't, against he ha' the widow,
To furnish household.
Sub.   Excellent, well thought on.
'Pray God he come.
Face.   I pray he keep away   60
Till our new business be o'erpast.
Sub.   But Face,
How camest thou by this secret Don?
Face.   A spirit
Brought me th'intelligence in a paper, here,
As I was conjuring yonder in my circle
For Surly: I ha' my flies abroad. Your bath
Is famous, Subtle, by my means. Sweet Doll,
You must go tune your virginal, no losing
O' the least time. And – do you hear? – good action:
Firk like a flounder, kiss like scallop, close;
And tickle him with thy mother-tongue. His great   70
Verdugoship has not a jot of language:
So much the easier to be cozened, my Dolly.
He will come here in a hired coach, obscure,
And our own coachman, whom I have sent as guide,
No creature else.   *One knocks.*
                Who's that?
Sub.   It i' not he?
Face. O no, not yet this hour.

Sub.   Who is't?
Doll. [*Looking out*]   Dapper,
    Your clerk.
Face.   God's will, then. Queen of Fairy,
    On with your tire; and Doctor, with your robes.
                                        [*Exit Doll.*]
    Let's dispatch him, for God's sake.
Sub.   'Twill be long.
Face. I warrant you, take but the cues I give you.   80
    It shall be brief enough. [*Looking out*] 'Slight, here are
        more!
    Abel and, I think, the angry boy, the heir,
    That fain would quarrel.
Sub.   And the widow?
Face.   No,
    Not that I see. Away.   [*Exit Subtle.*]
            O sir, you are welcome.

SCENE IV

[*Enter*] DAPPER.

[*Face.*] The Doctor is within, a-moving for you
    (I have had the most ado to win him to it);
    He swears you'll be the darling o' the dice;
    He never heard her Highness dote till now, he says.
    Your aunt has giv'n you the most gracious words
    That can be thought on.
Dap.   Shall I see her Grace?

[*Enter*] DRUGGER [*and*] KASTRIL.

Face. See her, and kiss her, too. What? Honest Nab!
    Hast brought the damask?
[*Dru.*]   No, sir, here's tobacco.
Face. 'Tis well done, Nab. Thou'lt bring the damask too?
Dru. Yes, here's the gentleman, Captain, Master Kastril,   10
    I have brought to see the Doctor.

Face.   Where's the widow?

Dru. Sir, as he likes, his sister, he says, shall come.

Face. O, is it so? 'Good time. Is your name Kastril, sir?

Kas. Ay, and the best o' the Kastrils, I'd be sorry else,
     By fifteen hundred a year. Where is this Doctor?
     My mad tobacco boy here tells me of one
     That can do things. Has he any skill?

Face.   Wherein, sir?

Kas. To carry a business, manage a quarrel fairly,
     Upon fit terms.

Face.   It seems, sir, you're but young
     About the town, that can make that a question!   20

Kas. Sir, not so young but I have heard some speech
     Of the angry boys, and seen 'em take tobacco,
     And in his shop; and I can take it too.
     And I would fain be one of 'em, and go down
     And practise i' the country.

Face.   Sir, for the duello,
     The Doctor, I assure you, shall inform you
     To the least shadow of a hair; and show you
     An instrument he has of his own making,
     Wherewith, no sooner shall you make report
     Of any quarrel, but he will take the height on't   30
     Most instantly, and tell in what degree
     Of safety it lies in, or mortality;
     And how it may be borne, whether in a right line
     Or a half circle, or may else be cast
     Into an angle blunt, if not acute:
     All this he will demonstrate. And then rules
     To give and take the lie by.

Kas.   How? To take it?

Face. Yes, in oblique, he'll show you, or in circle,
     But never in diameter. The whole town
     Study his theorems, and dispute them ordinarily   40
     At the eating academies.

Kas.   But does he teach
     Living by the wits, too?

Face.   Anything whatever.

You cannot think that subtlety, but he reads it.
He made me a captain. I was a stark pimp,
Just o' your standing, 'fore I met with him;
It i' not two months since. I'll tell you his method.
First, he will enter you at some ordinary.

Kas. No, I'll not come there. You shall pardon me.

Face.   For why,
     sir?

Kas. There's gaming there, and tricks.

Face.   Why, would you be
     A gallant, and not game?

Kas.   Ay, 'twill spend a man.   50

Face. Spend you? It will repair you, when you are spent.
     How do they live by their wits there, that have vented
     Six times your fortunes?

Kas.   What, three thousand a year!

Face. Aye, forty thousand.

Kas.   Are there such?

Face.   Ay, sir,
     And gallants, yet. Here's a young gentleman
     Is born to nothing, forty marks a year,
     Which I count nothing. He's to be initiated,
     And have a fly o' the Doctor. He will win you
     By unresistible luck, within this fortnight,
     Enough to buy a barony. They will set him   60
     Upmost at the groom-porter's all the Christmas!
     And for the whole year through at every place
     Where there is play, present him with the chair,
     The best attendance, the best drink, sometimes
     Two glasses of canary, and pay nothing;
     The purest linen, and the sharpest knife,
     The partridge next his trencher; and somewhere
     The dainty bed, in private, with the dainty.
     You shall ha' your ordinaries bid for him,
     As playhouses for a poet; and the master   70
     Pray him aloud to name what dish he affects,
     Which must be buttered shrimps; and those that drink

    To no mouth else, will drink to his, as being
    The goodly, president mouth of all the board.
Kas. Do you not gull one?
Face.   'Ods my life! Do you think it?
    You shall have a cast commander (can but get
    In credit with a glover or a spurrier
    For some two pair of either's ware, aforehand)
    Will, by most swift posts, dealing with him,
    Arrive at competent means to keep himself,   80
    His punk, and naked boy, in excellent fashion,
    And be admired for't.
Kas.   Will the Doctor teach this?
Face. He will do more, sir: when your land is gone
    (As men of spirit hate to keep earth long),
    In a vacation, when small money is stirring,
    And ordinaries suspended till the term,
    He'll show a perspective, where on one side
    You shall behold the faces and the persons
    Of all sufficient young heirs in town,
    Whose bonds are current for commodity;   90
    On th'other side, the merchants' forms, and others,
    That, without help of any second broker
    (Who would expect a share), will trust such parcels;
    In the third square, the very street and sign
    Where the commodity dwells, and does but wait
    To be delivered, be it pepper, soap,
    Hops or tobacco, oatmeal, woad or cheeses.
    All which you may so handle, to enjoy
    To your own use, and never stand obliged.
Kas. I' faith! Is he such a fellow?
Face.   Why, Nab here knows him. 100
    And then for making matches for rich widows,
    Young gentlewomen, heirs, the fortunatest man!
    He's sent to, far and near, all over England,
    To have his counsel, and to know their fortunes.
Kas. God's will, my suster shall see him.
Face.   I'll tell you, sir,

What he did tell me of Nab. It's a strange thing!
(By the way you must eat no cheese, Nab, it breeds
  melancholy:
And that same melancholy breeds worms; but pass it.)
He told me, honest Nab here was ne'er at tavern
But once in's life!

Dru.   Truth, and no more I was not.   110

Face. And then he was so sick –

Dru.   Could he tell you that, too?

Face. How should I know it?

Dru.   In troth we had been a-shooting,
And had a piece of fat ram-mutton to supper,
That lay so heavy o' my stomach –

Face.   And he has no head
To bear any wine; for what with the noise o' the fiddlers,
And care of his shop, for he dares keep no servants –

Dru. My head did so ache –

Face.   As he was fain to be brought home,
The Doctor told me. And then a good old woman –

Dru. (Yes faith, she dwells in Seacoal Lane) did cure me
With sodden ale and pellitory o' the wall;   120
Cost me but two pence. I had another sickness
Was worse than that.

Face.   Ay, that was with the grief
Thou took'st for being 'sessed at eighteen pence
For the waterwork.

Dru.   In truth, and it was like
T'have cost me almost my life.

Face.   Thy hair went off?

Dru. Yes, sir, 'twas done for spite.

Face.   Nay, so says the Doctor.

Kas. 'Pray thee, tobacco-boy, go fetch my suster.
I'll see this learned boy before I go,
And so shall she.

Face.   Sir, he is busy now;
But, if you have a sister to fetch hither,   130
Perhaps your own pains may command her sooner,

And he by that time will be free.

Kas.   I go.   [*Exit.*]

Face. Drugger, she's thine; the damask.   [*Exit Drugger.*]
    [*Aside*]   Subtle and I
    Must wrestle for her. – Come on, Master Dapper;
    You see how I turn clients here away
    To give your cause dispatch. Ha' you performed
    The ceremonies were enjoined you?

Dap.   Yes, o' the vinegar,
    And the clean shirt.

Face.   'Tis well: that shirt may do you
    More worship than you think. Your aunt's a-fire,
    But that she will not show it, t'have a sight on you. 140
    Ha' you provided for her Grace's servants?

Dap. Yes, here are six score Edward shillings –

Face.   Good.

Dap. And an old Harry's sovereign –

Face.   Very good.

Dap. And three James shillings, and an Elizabeth groat:
    Just twenty nobles.

Face.   O, you are too just.
    I would you had had the other noble in Maries.

Dap. I have some Philip and Maries.

Face.   Ay, those same
    Are best of all. Where are they? Hark, the Doctor.

SCENE V

[*Enter*] SUBTLE *disguised like a Priest of Fairy.*

[*Sub.*] Is yet her Grace's cousin come?

Face.   He is come.

Sub. And is he fasting?

Face.   Yes.

Sub.   And hath cried 'hum'?

Face. 'Thrice', you must answer.

Dap.   Thrice.
Sub.   And as oft 'buzz'?
Face. If you have, say.
Dap.   I have.
Sub.   Then to her, coz!
    Hoping that he hath vinegared his senses
    As he was bid, the Fairy Queen dispenses,
    By me, this robe, the petticoat of Fortune;
    Which that he straight put on, she doth importune.
    And though to Fortune near be her petticoat,
    Yet nearer is her smock, the Queen doth note;   10
    And therefore, ev'n of that a piece she hath sent,
    Which, being a child, to wrap him in, was rent;
    And prays him, for a scarf he now will wear it,
    With as much love as then her Grace did tear it,
    About his eyes, to show he is fortunate;
                              They blind him with a rag.
    And, trusting unto her to make his state,
    He'll throw away all wordly pelf about him:
    Which that he will perform, she doth not doubt him.
Face. She need not doubt him, sir. Alas, he has nothing
    But what he will part withal, as willingly,   20
    Upon her Grace's word – throw away your purse –
    As she would ask it: – handkerchiefs and all –
                         He throws away, as they bid him.
    She cannot bid that thing, but he'll obey.
    If you have a ring about you, cast it off,
    Or a silver seal at your wrist: her Grace will send
    Her fairies here to search you, therefore deal
    Directly with her Highness. If they find
    That you conceal a mite, you are undone.
Dap. Truly, there's all.
Face.   All what?
Dap.   My money, truly.
Face. Keep nothing that is transitory about you.   30
    [*To Subtle*] Bid Doll play music.

        DOLL *enters with a cithern: they pinch him.*

                             Look, the elves are come

   To pinch you if you tell not truth. Advise you.

Dap. O, I have a paper with a spur-rial in't.

Face.   *Ti, ti.*

   They knew't, they say.

Sub.   *Ti, ti, ti, ti.* He has more yet.

Face. Ti, ti-ti-ti. I' the t'other pocket?

Sub.   *Titi, titi, titi, titi.*

   They must pinch him, or he will never confess, they say.

Dap. O, O!

Face.   Nay, 'pray you hold. He is her Grace's nephew.

   Ti, ti, ti? What care you? Good faith, you shall care.

   Deal plainly, sir, and shame the fairies. Show

   You are an innocent.

Dap.   By this good light, I ha' nothing.   40

Sub. Ti ti, ti ti to ta. He does equivocate, she says.

   Ti, ti do ti, ti ti do, ti da. And swears by the light, when he

     is blinded.

Dap. By this good dark, I ha' nothing but a half-crown

   Of gold about my wrist, that my love gave me,

   And a leaden heart I wore sin' she forsook me.

                                   [Exit Doll.]

Face. I thought 'twas something. And would you incur

   Your aunt's displeasure for these trifles? Come,

   I had rather you had thrown away twenty half-crowns.

   You may wear your leaden heart still.

                   [Enter] DOLL.

                            How now?

Sub. What news, Doll?

Doll.   Yonder's your knight, Sir Mammon.   50

Face. God's lid, we never thought of him till now.

   Where is he?

Doll.   Here, hard by. He's at the door.

Sub. [To Face] And you are not ready, now? Doll, get his suit.

   He must not be sent back.   *[Exit Doll.]*

Face.   O, by no means.

What shall we do with this same puffin here,
Now he's o' the spit?
Sub.   Why, lay him back awhile,
With some device. – *Ti, ti ti, ti ti ti.*

[*Enter* DOLL.]

                    Would her Grace speak with me?
I come. – Help, Doll.   [*Doll helps Face into his suit.*]
Face. (*He speaks through the keyhole, the other* [*Mammon*] *knocking.*)
                    Who's there? Sir Epicure;
My master's i' the way. Please you to walk
Three or four turns, but till his back be turned,   60
And I am for you. – Quickly, Doll.
Sub.   Her Grace
Commends her kindly to you, Master Dapper.
Dap. I long to see her Grace.
Sub.   She now is set
At dinner in her bed, and she has sent you,
From her own private trencher, a dead mouse
And a piece of gingerbread, to be merry withal,
And stay your stomach lest you faint with fasting;
Yet if you could hold out till she saw you, she says,
It would be better for you.
Face.   Sir, he shall
Hold out, and 'twere this two hours, for her
    Highness;   70
I can assure you that. We will not lose
All we ha' done –
Sub.   He must nor see nor speak
To anybody till then.
Face.   For that we'll put, sir,
A stay in's mouth.
Sub.   Of what?
Face.   Of gingerbread.
Make you it fit. He that hath pleased her Grace
Thus far, shall not now crinkle for a little.
Gape, sir, and let him fit you.

Sub.　　　　　　　Where shall we now
　　Bestow him?
Doll.　　　　I' the privy.
Sub.　　　　　　　Come along, sir,
　　I now must show you Fortune's privy lodgings.
Face. Are they perfumed, and his bath ready?
Sub.　　　　　　　All,　　　80
　　Only the fumigation's somewhat strong.
Face. Sir Epicure, I am yours, sir, by and by.
　　　　　　　　　[*Exeunt Subtle and Doll with Dapper.*]

ACT IV

SCENE I

[Enter] MAMMON.

[Face.] O, sir, you're come i' the only, finest time –
Mam. Where's master?
Face.   Now preparing for projection, sir.
　Your stuff will b'all changed shortly.
Mam.   Into gold?
Face. To gold and silver, sir.
Mam.   Silver I care not for.
Face. Yes, sir, a little to give beggars.
Mam.   Where's the lady?
Face. At hand here. I ha' told her such brave things o' you,
　Touching your bounty and your noble spirit –
Mam.   Hast thou?
Face. As she is almost in her fit to see you.
　But, good sir, no divinity i' your conference,
　For fear of putting her in rage –
Mam.   I warrant thee.   10
Face. Six men will not hold her down. And then,
　If the old man should hear or see you –
Mam.   Fear not.
Face. The very house, sir, would run mad. You know it,
　How scrupulous he is, and violent
　'Gainst the least act of sin. Physic or mathematics,
　Poetry, state, or bawdry (as I told you)
　She will endure, and never startle; but
　No word of controversy.
Mam.   I am schooled, good Ulen.

Face. And you must praise her house, remember that,
      And her nobility.
Mam.   Let me alone: 20
      No herald, no, nor antiquary, Lungs,
      Shall do it better. Go.
Face. [*Aside*]   Why, this is yet
      A kind of modern happiness, to have
      Doll Common for a great lady.   [*Exit.*]
Mam.   Now, Epicure,
      Heighten thyself; talk to her, all in gold;
      Rain her as many showers as Jove did drops
      Unto his Danae; show the god a miser
      Compared with Mammon. What? The stone will do't.
      She shall feel gold, taste gold, hear gold, sleep gold;
      Nay, we will *concumbere* gold. I will be puissant,   30
      And mighty in my talk to her!

                    [*Enter* FACE *with* DOLL.]

                              Here she comes.
Face. [*Aside*] To him, Doll, suckle him. – This is the noble
      knight
      I told your ladyship –
Mam.   Madam, with your pardon,
      I kiss your vesture.
Doll.   Sir, I were uncivil
      If I would suffer that: my lip to you, sir.
Mam. I hope my lord your brother be in health, lady?
Doll. My lord my brother is, though I no lady, sir.
Face. [*Aside*] Well said, my Guinea-bird.
Mam.   Right noble madam –
Face. [*Aside*] O, we shall have most fierce idolatry!
Mam. 'Tis your prerogative.
Doll.   Rather your courtesy.   40
Mam. Were there nought else t'enlarge your virtues to me,
      These answers speak your breeding and your blood.
Doll. Blood we boast none, sir: a poor baron's daughter.
Mam. Poor! And gat you? Profane not. Had your father

Slept all the happy remnant of his life
After that act, lain but there still, and panted,
He'd done enough to make himself, his issue,
And his posterity noble.

Doll.   Sir, although
We may be said to want the gilt and trappings,
The dress of honour, yet we strive to keep   50
The seeds and the materials.

Mam.   I do see
The old ingredient, virtue, was not lost,
Nor the drug, money, used to make your compound.
There is a strange nobility i' your eye,
This lip, that chin! Methinks you do resemble
One o' the Austriac princes.

Face. [*Aside*]   Very like,
Her father was an Irish costermonger.

Mam. The house of Valois just had such a nose,
And such a forehead yet the Medici
Of Florence boast.

Doll.   Troth, and I have been likened   60
To all these princes.

Face. [*Aside*]   I'll be sworn, I heard it.

Mam. I know not how! It is not any one,
But e'en the very choice of all their features.

Face. [*Aside*] I'll in, and laugh.   [*Exit.*]

Mam.   A certain touch, or air,
That sparkles a divinity beyond
An earthly beauty! ·

Doll.   O, you play the courtier.

Mam. Good lady, gi' me leave –

Doll.   In faith, I may not,
To mock me, sir.

Mam.   To burn i' this sweet flame:
The Phoenix never knew a nobler death.

Doll. Nay, now you court the courtier, and destroy   70
What you would build. This art, sir, i' your words,
Calls your whole faith in question.

Mam.   By my soul –
Doll. Nay, oaths are made o' the same air, sir.
Mam.   Nature
    Never bestowed upon mortality
    A more unblamed, a more harmonious feature:
    She played the stepdame in all faces else.
    Sweet madam, le' me be particular –
Doll. Particular, sir? I pray you, know your distance.
Mam. In no ill sense, sweet lady, but to ask
    How your fair graces pass the hours? I see   80
    You're lodged here i' the house of a rare man,
    An excellent artist; but what's that to you?
Doll. Yes, sir. I study here the mathematics
    And distillation.
Mam.   O, I cry your pardon.
    He's a divine instructor! Can extract
    The souls of all things, by his art; call all
    The virtues and the miracles of the sun
    Into a temperate furnace; teach dull nature
    What her own forces are. A man the Emp'ror
    Has courted above Kelly; sent his medals   90
    And chains t'invite him.
Doll.   Ay, and for his physic, sir –
Mam. Above the art of Aesculapius,
    That drew the envy of the Thunderer!
    I know all this, and more.
Doll.   Troth, I am taken, sir,
    Whole, with these studies that contemplate nature.
Mam. It is a noble humour. But this form
    Was not intended to so dark a use!
    Had you been crooked, foul, of some coarse mould,
    A cloister had done well; but such a feature
    That might stand up the glory of a kingdom,   100
    To live recluse is a mere solecism,
    Though in a nunnery! It must not be.
    I muse, my lord your brother will permit it!
    You should spend half my land first, were I he.

Does not this diamond better on my finger,
Than i' the quarry?
Doll.   Yes.
Mam.   Why, you are like it.
You were created, lady, for the light!
Here, you shall wear it: take it, the first pledge
Of what I speak, to bind you to believe me.
Doll. In chains of adamant?
Mam.   Yes, the strongest bands.   110
And take a secret, too. Here by your side
Doth stand, this hour, the happiest man in Europe.
Doll. You are contented, sir?
Mam.   Nay, in true being:
The envy of princes and the fear of states.
Doll. Say you so, Sir Epicure?
Mam.   Yes, and thou shalt prove it,
Daughter of honour. I have cast mine eye
Upon thy form, and I will rear this beauty
Above all styles.
Doll.   You mean no treason, sir?
Mam. No, I will take away that jealousy.
I am the lord of the philosopher's stone,   120
And thou the lady.
Doll.   How, sir! Ha' you that?
Mam. I am the master of the mastery.
This day the good old wretch here o' the house
Has made it for us. Now he's at projection.
Think, therefore, thy first wish now: let me hear it,
And it shall rain into thy lap, no shower,
But floods of gold, whole cataracts, a deluge,
To get a nation on thee!
Doll.   You are pleased, sir,
To work on the ambition of our sex.
Mam. I am pleased the glory of her sex should know   130
This nook here of the Friars is no climate
For her to live obscurely in, to learn
Physic and surgery for the constable's wife

Of some odd hundred in Essex; but come forth
And taste the air of palaces; eat, drink
The toils of emp'rics, and their boasted practice;
Tincture of pearl, and coral, gold, and amber;
Be seen at feasts and triumphs; have it asked
What miracle she is; set all the eyes
Of court a-fire, like a burning-glass,   140
And work 'em into cinders, when the jewels
Of twenty states adorn thee, and the light
Strikes out the stars: that, when thy name is mentioned,
Queens may look pale; and, we but showing our love,
Nero's Poppaea may be lost in story!
Thus will we have it.

Doll.   I could well consent, sir.
But in a monarchy, how will this be?
The Prince will soon take notice, and both seize
You and your stone, it being a wealth unfit
For any private subject.

Mam.   If he knew it.   150

Doll. Yourself do boast it, sir.

Mam.   To thee, my life.

Doll. O, but beware, sir! You may come to end
The remnant of your days in a loathed prison
By speaking of it.

Mam.   'Tis no idle fear!
We'll therefore go with all, my girl, and live
In a free state, where we will eat our mullets
Soused in high-country wines, sup pheasants' eggs,
And have our cockles boiled in silver shells;
Our shrimps to swim again as when they lived,
In a rare butter made of dolphin's milk,   160
Whose cream does look like opals; and, with these
Delicate meats, set ourselves high for pleasure,
And take us down again, and then renew
Our youth and strength with drinking the elixir,
And so enjoy a perpetuity
Of life and lust. And thou shalt ha' thy wardrobe

Richer than Nature's, still, to change thyself,
And vary oft'ner for thy pride than she,
Or Art, her wise and almost-equal servant.

[*Enter* FACE.]

Face. Sir, you are too loud. I hear you, every word,   170
    Into the laboratory. Some fitter place:
    The garden, or great chamber above. How like you her?
Mam. Excellent, Lungs! There's for thee. [*Giving money*]
Face. But do you hear?
Face. Good sir, beware, no mention of the Rabbins.
Mam. We think not on 'em.
Face.   O, it is well, sir.

                        [*Exeunt Doll and Mammon.*]
                        Subtle!

SCENE II

[*Enter*] SUBTLE.

[*Face.*] Dost thou not laugh?
Sub.   Yes. Are they gone?
Face.   All's clear.
Sub. The widow is come.
Face.   And your quarrelling disciple?
Sub. Ay.
Face.   I must to my captainship again, then.
Sub. Stay, bring 'em in first.
Face.   So I meant. What is she?
    A bonnibel?
Sub.   I know not.
Face.   We'll draw lots.
    You'll stand to that?
Sub.   What else?
Face.   O, for a suit
    To fall now like a curtain, flap!
Sub.   To th'door, man.

Face. You'll ha' the first kiss, 'cause I am not ready.

Sub. [*Aside*] Yes, and perhaps hit you through both the nostrils.

Face. Who would you speak with?

[*Enter*] KASTRIL, DAME PLIANT.

Kas.   Where's the Captain?

Face.   Gone, sir,   10
    About some business.

Kas.   Gone?

Face.   He'll return straight.
    But Master Doctor, his lieutenant, is here.   [*Exit.*]

Sub. Come near, my worshipful boy, my *terrae fili*,
    That is, my boy of land; make thy approaches.
    Welcome, I know thy lusts and thy desires,
    And I will serve and satisfy 'em. Begin,
    Charge me from thence, or thence, or in this line;
    Here is my centre: ground thy quarrel.

Kas.   You lie.

Sub. How, child of wrath and anger! The loud lie?
    For what, my sudden boy?

Kas.   Nay, that look you to: 20
    I am aforehand.

Sub.   O, this's no true grammar,
    And as ill logic! You must render causes, child,
    Your first and second intentions; know your canons
    And your divisions, moods, degrees, and differences,
    Your predicaments, substance, and accident,
    Series extern, and intern, with their causes
    Efficient, material, formal, final,
    And ha' your elements perfect —

Kas.   What is this,
    The angry tongue he talks in?

Sub.   That false precept
    Of being aforehand has deceived a number,   30
    And made 'em enter quarrels oftentimes
    Before they were aware, and afterward,
    Against their wills.

Kas.   How must I do then, sir?

Sub. I cry this lady mercy. She should first
    Have been saluted. I do call you lady,
    Because you are to be one ere't be long,
    My soft and buxom widow.   *He kisses her.*
Kas.   Is she, i' faith?
Sub. Yes, or my art is an egregious liar.
Kas. How know you?
Sub.   By inspection on her forehead,
    And subtlety of her lip, which must be tasted   40
    Often, to make a judgement.   *He kisses her again.*
                'Slight, she melts
    Like a myrobalane! Here is yet a line
    In rivo frontis tells me he is no knight.
Pli. What is he then, sir?
Sub.   Let me see your hand.
    O, your *linea Fortunae* makes it plain,
    And *stella*, here, *in monte Veneris*;
    But most of all, *junctura annularis.*
    He is a soldier or a man of art, lady,
    But shall have some great honour shortly.
Pli.   Brother,
    He's a rare man, believe me!
Kas.   Hold your peace.   50

                [*Enter* FACE.]

    Here comes the t'other rare man. 'Save you, Captain.
Face. Good Master Kastril. Is this your sister?
Kas.   Ay, sir.
    Please you to kuss her, and be proud to know her?
Face. I shall be proud to know you, lady.
Pli.   Brother,
    He calls me lady, too.
Kas.   Ay, peace. I heard it.
Face. [*Aside to Subtle*] The Count is come.
Sub. [*Aside*]   Where is he?
Face. [*Aside*]   At the door.
Sub. [*Aside*] Why, you must entertain him.

Face. [*Aside*]   What'll you do
      With these the while?
Sub. [*Aside*]   Why, have 'em up, and show 'em
      Some fustian book, or the dark glass.
Face. [*Aside*]   'Fore God,
      She is a delicate dabchick! I must have her.   [*Exit.*] 60
Sub. [*Aside*] Must you? Ay, if your fortune will, you must.
      [*To Kastril*] Come sir, the Captain will come to us presently.
      I'll ha' you to my chamber of demonstrations,
      Where I'll show you both the grammar and logic
      And rhetoric of quarrelling, my whole method
      Drawn out in tables; and my instrument,
      That hath the several scale upon't, shall make you
      Able to quarrel at a straw's breadth, by moonlight.
      And, lady, I'll have you look in a glass
      Some half an hour, but to clear your eyesight   70
      Against you see your fortune; which is greater
      Than I may judge upon the sudden, trust me.   [*Exeunt.*]

.

SCENE III

[*Enter*] FACE.

[*Face.*] Where are you, Doctor?
Sub. [*Within*]   I'll come to you presently.
Face. I will ha' this same widow, now I ha' seen her,
      On any composition.

[*Enter*] SUBTLE.

Sub.   What do you say?
Face. Ha' you disposed of them?
Sub.   I ha' sent 'em up.
Face. Subtle, in troth, I needs must have this widow.
Sub. Is that the matter?
Face.   Nay, but hear me.

Sub.   Go to,
    If you rebel once, Doll shall know it all.
    Therefore be quiet, and obey your chance.
Face. Nay, thou art so violent now – do but conceive:
    Thou art old, and canst not serve –
Sub.   Who cannot? I?   10
    'Slight, I will serve her with thee, for a –
Face.   Nay,
    But understand: I'll gi' you composition.
Sub. I will not treat with thee: what, sell my fortune?
    'Tis better than my birthright. Do not murmur.
    Win her, and carry her. If you grumble, Doll
    Knows it directly.
Face.   Well, sir, I am silent.
    Will you go help to fetch in Don, in state?   [*Exit.*]
Sub. I follow you, sir. We must keep Face in awe,
    Or he will overlook us like a tyrant.

       [*Enter*] SURLY *like a Spaniard* [*and* FACE].

    Brain of a tailor! Who comes here? Don John!   20
Sur. Señores, beso las manos, a vuestras mercedes.
Sub. Would you had stooped a little, and kissed our *anos.*
Face. Peace, Subtle.
Sub.   Stab me! I shall never hold, man.
    He looks in that deep ruff like a head in a platter,
    Served in by a short cloak upon two trestles!
Face. Or what do you say to a collar of brawn, cut down
    Beneath the souse, and wriggled with a knife?
Sub. 'Slud, he does look too fat to be a Spaniard.
Face. Perhaps some Fleming or some Hollander got him
    In D'Alva's time: Count Egmont's bastard.
Sub.   Don,   30
    Your scurvy, yellow, Madrid face is welcome.
Sur. Gracias.
Sub.   He speaks out of a fortification.
    'Pray God he ha' no squibs in those deep sets.
Sur. ¡*Por dios, señores, muy linda casa!*

Sub. What says he?

Face.   Praises the house, I think.
  I know no more but's action.

Sub.   Yes, the *casa,*
  My precious Diego, will prove fair enough
  To cozen you in. Do you mark? You shall
  Be cozened, Diego.

Face.   Cozened, do you see,
  My worthy Donzel, cozened.

Sur.   *Entiendo.*   40

Sub. Do you intend it? So do we, dear Don.
  Have you brought pistolets or portagues,
  My solemn Don?   *He feels his pockets.*
  [*To Face*]   Dost thou feel any?

Face. [*To Subtle*]   Full.

Sub. You shall be emptied, Don; pumpèd and drawn
  Dry, as they say.

Face.   Milkèd, in troth, sweet Don.

Sub. See all the monsters; the great lion of all, Don.

Sur. *¿Con licencia, se puede ver a esta señora?*

Sub. What talks he now?

Face.   O' the *señora.*

Sub.   O, Don,
  That is the lioness, which you shall see
  Also, my Don.

Face.   'Slid, Subtle, how shall we do?   50

Sub. For what?

Face.   Why, Doll's employed, you know.

Sub.   That's true!
  'Fore heaven I know not; he must stay, that's all.

Face. Stay? That he must not, by no means.

Sub.   No, why?

Face. Unless you'll mar all. 'Slight, he'll suspect it.
  And then he will not pay, not half so well.
  This is a travelled punk-master, and does know
  All the delays; a notable hot rascal,
  And looks already rampant.

Sub.   'Sdeath, and Mammon
    Must not be troubled.

Face.   Mammon? In no case!

Sub. What shall we do then?

Face.   Think: you must be sudden.   60

Sur. Entiendo, que la señora es tan hermosa, que codicio tan a verla,
    como la bien aventuranza de mi vida.

Face. Mi vida? 'Slid, Subtle, he puts me in mind o' the widow.
    What dost thou say to draw her to't, ha?
    And tell her it is her fortune. All our venture
    Now lies upon't. It is but one man more,
    Which on's chance to have her; and beside,
    There is no maidenhead to be feared or lost.
    What dost thou think on't, Subtle?

Sub.   Who, I? Why –

Face. The credit of our house too is engaged.   70

Sub. You made me an offer for my share erewhile.
    What wilt thou gi' me, i' faith?

Face.   O, by that light,
    I'll not buy now. You know your doom to me.
    E'en take your lot, obey your chance, sir; win her
    And wear her out for me.

Sub.   'Slight, I'll not work her then.

Face. It is the common cause, therefore bethink you.
    Doll else must know it, as you said.

Sub.   I care not.

Sur. Señores, ¿por qué se tarda tanto?

Sub. Faith, I am not fit, I am old.

Face.   That's now no reason, sir.

Sur. Puede ser de hacer burla de mi amor.   80

Face. You hear the Don, too? By this air, I call,
    And loose the hinges. Doll!

Sub.   A plague of hell –

Face. Will you then do?

Sub.   You're a terrible rogue!
    I'll think of this. Will you, sir, call the widow?

Face. Yes, and I'll take her too, with all her faults,
    Now I do think on't better.

Sub.   With all my heart, sir.
　　Am I discharged o' the lot?
Face.   As you please.
Sub.   Hands.
Face. Remember now, that upon any change
　　You never claim her.
Sub.   Much good joy and health to you, sir.
　　Marry a whore? Fate, let me wed a witch first.   90
Sur. Por estas honradas barbas –
Sub.   He swears by his beard.
　　Dispatch, and call the brother too.   [*Exit Face.*]
Sur. Tengo duda, señores, que no me hagan alguna traycion.
Sub. How, issue on? Yes, *presto, señor.* Please you
　　Enthratha the *chambratha,* worthy Don;
　　Where if it please the Fates, in your *bathada*
　　You shall be soaked, and stroked, and tubbed, and rubbed,
　　And scrubbed, and fubbed, dear Don, before you go.
　　You shall, in faith, my scurvy baboon Don,
　　Be curried, clawed, and flawed, and tawed, indeed.   100
　　I will the heartilier go about it now,
　　And make the widow a punk, so much the sooner,
　　To be revenged on this impetuous Face:
　　The quickly doing of it is the grace.   [*Exeunt.*]

SCENE IV

[*Enter*] FACE, KASTRIL [*and*] DAME PLIANT.

[*Face.*] Come, lady. I knew the Doctor would not leave
　　Till he had found the very nick of her fortune.
Kas. To be a Countess, say you?
Face.   A Spanish Countess, sir.
Pli. Why, is that better than an English Countess?
Face. Better? 'Slight, make you that a question, lady?
Kas. Nay, she is a fool, Captain: you must pardon her.
Face. Ask from your courtier, to your inns-of-court-man,
　　To your mere milliner: they will tell you all,

Your Spanish jennet is the best horse; your Spanish
Stoop is the best garb; your Spanish beard   10
Is the best cut; your Spanish ruffs are the best
Wear; your Spanish pavan the best dance;
Your Spanish titillation in a glove
The best perfume; and, for your Spanish pike
And Spanish blade, let your poor Captain speak.
Here comes the Doctor.

[Enter] SUBTLE.

Sub.   My most honoured lady
(For so I am now to style you, having found
By this my scheme, you are to undergo
An honourable fortune very shortly),
What will you say now, if some –
Face.   I ha' told her all, sir,   20
And her right worshipful brother here, that she shall be
A Countess: do not delay 'em, sir. A Spanish Countess!
Sub. Still, my scarce worshipful Captain, you can keep
No secret. Well, since he has told you, madam,
Do you forgive him, and I do.
Kas.   She shall do that, sir.
I'll look to't, 'tis my charge.
Sub.   Well then. Nought rests
But that she fit her love now to her fortune.
Pli. Truly, I shall never brook a Spaniard.
Sub.   No?
Pli. Never sin' eighty-eight could I abide 'em,
And that was some three year afore I was born, in truth. 30
Sub. Come, you must love him, or be miserable:
Choose which you will.
Face.   By this good rush, persuade her;
She will cry strawberries else within this twelvemonth.
Sub. Nay, shads and mackerel, which is worse.
Face.   Indeed, sir?
Kas. God's lid, you shall love him, or I'll kick you.
Pli.   Why,

I'll do as you will ha' me, brother.

Kas.   Do,

Or by this hand, I'll maul you.

Face.   Nay, good sir,

Be not so fierce.

Sub.   No, my enragèd child,

She will be ruled. What, when she comes to taste

The pleasures of a Countess! To be courted –   40

Face. And kissed, and ruffled!

Sub.   Ay, behind the hangings.

Face. And then come forth in pomp!

Sub.   And know her state!

Face. Of keeping all th'idolators o' the chamber

Barer to her than at their prayers!

Sub.   Is served

Upon the knee!

Face.   And has her pages, ushers,

Footmen and coaches –

                              Her six mares –

Face.   Nay, eight!

Sub. To hurry her through London to th'Exchange,

Bedlam, the China-houses –

Face.   Yes, and have

The citizens gape at her, and praise her tires!

And my lord's goose-turd bands, that rides with her!   50

Kas. Most brave! By this hand, you are not my suster

If you refuse.

Pli.   I will not refuse, brother.

[*Enter*] SURLY.

Sur. ¿Qué es esto, señores, que no se venga?

¡Esta tardanza me mata!

Face.   It is the Count come!

The Doctor knew he would be here, by his art.

Sub. En gallanta madama, Don! Gallantissima!

Sur. ¡Por todos los dioses, la más acabada hermosura, que he visto en

mi vida!

Face. Is't not a gallant language that they speak?

Kas. An admirable language! Is't not French?   60

Face. No, Spanish, sir.

Kas.   It goes like law-French,
And that, they say, is the courtliest language.

Face.   List, sir.

Sur. *El sol ha perdido su lumbre, con el resplandor, que trae esta
    dama. ¡Válgame dios!*

Face. He admires your sister.

Kas.   Must not she make curtsy?

Sub. 'Ods will, she must go to him, man, and kiss him!
It is the Spanish fashion for the women
To make first court.

Face.   'Tis true he tells you, sir:
His art knows all.

Sur.   ¿*Por qué no se acude?*

Kas. He speaks to her, I think?

Face.   That he does, sir.   70

Sur. *Por el amor de dios, ¿qué es esto que se tarda?*

Kas. Nay, see, she will not understand him! Gull!
Noddy!

Pli.   What say you, brother?

Kas.   Ass, my suster!
Go kuss him, as the cunning man would ha' you;
I'll thrust a pin i' your buttocks else.

Face.   O, no, sir.

Sur. *Señora mía, mi persona muy indigna está a llegar a tanta
    hermosura.*

Face. Does he not use her bravely?

Kas.   Bravely, i' faith!

Face. Nay, he will use her better.

Kas.   Do you think so?

Sur. *Señora, si será servida, entremos.*   80

                    [*Exeunt Surly and Pliant.*]

Kas. Where does he carry her?

Face.   Into the garden, sir;
Take you no thought. I must interpret for her.

Sub. [*To Face*] Give Doll the word.   [*Exit Face.*]
                     Come, my fierce child,
   advance;
   We'll to our quarrelling lesson again.
Kas.   Agreed.
   I love a Spanish boy with all my heart.
Sub. Nay, and by this means, sir, you shall be brother
   To a great Count.
Kas.   Ay, I knew that at first.
   This match will advance the house of the Kastrils.
Sub. 'Pray God your sister prove but pliant.
Kas.   Why,
   Her name is so, by her other husband.
Sub.   How!   90
Kas. The Widow Pliant. Knew you not that?
Sub.   No, faith, sir.
   Yet by erection of her figure I guessed it.
   Come let's go practise.
Kas.   Yes, but do you think, Doctor,
   I e'er shall quarrel well?
Sub.   I warrant you.   [*Exeunt.*]

SCENE V

[*Enter*] DOLL *in her fit of talking* [*and*] MAMMON.

[*Doll.*] For after Alexander's death –
Mam.   Good lady –
Doll. That Perdicas and Antigonus were slain,
   The two that stood, Seleuc' and Ptolemy –
Mam. Madam –
Doll.   Make up the two legs, and the fourth Beast.
   That was Gog-north and Egypt-south, which after
   Was called Gog Iron-leg and South Iron-leg –
Mam.   Lady –
Doll. And then Gog-hornèd. So was Egypt, too.

Then Egypt Clay-leg and Gog Clay-leg –
Mam.   Sweet madam –
Doll. And last Gog-dust and Egypt-dust, which fall
   In the last link of the fourth chain. And these   10
   Be stars in story, which none see or look at –
Mam. What shall I do?
Doll.   For, as he says, except
   We call the Rabbins and the heathen Greeks –
Mam. Dear lady –
Doll.   To come from Salem and from Athens,
   And teach the people of Great Britain –

                    [*Enter* FACE.]

Face.   What's the matter,
      sir?
Doll. To speak the tongue of Eber, and Javan –
Mam.   O,
   She's in her fit.
Doll.   We shall know nothing –
Face.   Death, sir,
   We are undone!
Doll.   Where then a learned linguist
   Shall see the ancient used communion
   Of vowels and consonants –
Face.   My master will hear!   20
Doll. A wisdom which Pythagoras held most high –
Mam. Sweet honourable lady –
Doll.   To comprise
   All sounds of voices in few marks of letters –
Face. Nay, you must never hope to lay her now.

                    They speak together.

Doll. And so we may arrive	*Face.* How did you put her into't?
by Talmud skill	*Mam.* Alas I talked
And profane Greek to	Of a fifth monarchy I would
raise the building up	erect
Of Helen's house against	With the philosopher's stone
the Ismaelite,	(by chance) and she

King of Thogarma, and
   his Habergions
Brimstony, blue, and
   fiery; and the force

Of King Abaddon, and
   the Beast of Cittim;
Which Rabbi David
   Kimchi, Onkelos,
And Aben-Ezra do
   interpret Rome.

Falls on the four other, straight.
Face.   Out of Broughton!
   I told you so. 'Slid, stop her
   mouth.
Mam   Is't best?
Face. She'll never leave else. If
   the old man hear her,   30
   We are but faeces, ashes.
Sub. [*Within*] What's to do there?
Face. O, we are lost! Now she
   hears him, she is quiet.

Upon SUBTLE's *entry they disperse.* [*Exeunt Face and Doll.*]

Mam. Where shall I hide me?
Sub.   How! What sight is here!
   Close deeds of darkness, and that shun the light!
   Bring him again. Who is he? What, my son!
   O, I have lived too long.
Mam.   Nay, good, dear Father,
   There was no unchaste purpose.
Sub.   Not? And flee me,
   When I come in?
Mam.   That was my error.
Sub.   Error?
   Guilt, guilt, my son! Give it the right name. No marvel
   If I found check in our great work within,   40
   When such affairs as these were managing!
Mam. Why, have you so?
Sub.   It has stood still this half-hour,
   And all the rest of our less works gone back.
   Where is the instrument of wickedness,
   My lewd false drudge?
Mam.   Nay, good sir, blame not him.
   Believe me, 'twas against his will or knowledge.
   I saw her by chance.
Sub.   Will you commit more sin,
   T'excuse a varlet?
Mam.   By my hope, 'tis true, sir.

Sub. Nay, then I wonder less, if you, for whom
    The blessing was prepared, would so tempt heaven,   50
    And lose your fortunes.
Mam.   Why, sir?
Sub.   This'll retard
    The work a month at least.
Mam.   Why, if it do,
    What remedy? But think it not, good Father:
    Our purposes were honest.
Sub.   As they were,
    So the reward will prove.   *A great crack and noise within.*
                  How now! Ay me.
    God and all saints be good to us. What's that?

               [*Enter* FACE.]

Face. O sir, we are defeated! All the works
    Are flown *in fumo*: every glass is burst;
    Furnace and all rent down, as if a bolt
    Of thunder had been driven through the house!   60
    Retorts, receivers, pelicans, bolt-heads,
    All struck in shivers!   *Subtle falls down as in a swoon.*
              Help, good sir! Alas,
    Coldness and death invades him. Nay, Sir Mammon,
    Do the fair offices of a man! You stand
    As you were readier to depart than he.   *One knocks.*
    Who's there? [*Looking out*] My lord her brother is come.
Mam.   Ha, Lungs?
Face. His coach is at the door. Avoid his sight,
    For he's as furious as his sister is mad.
Mam. Alas!
Face.   My brain is quite undone with the fume, sir;
    I ne'er must hope to be mine own man again.   70
Mam. Is all lost, Lungs? Will nothing be preserved
    Of all our cost?
Face.   Faith, very little, sir.
    A peck of coals or so, which is cold comfort, sir.
Mam. O my voluptuous mind! I am justly punished.

Face. And so am I, sir.

Mam.   Cast from all my hopes –

Face. Nay, certainties, sir.

Mam.   By mine own base affections.

            Subtle seems come to himself.

Sub. O, the curst fruits of vice and lust!

Mam.   Good Father,

  It was my sin. Forgive it.

Sub.   Hangs my roof

  Over us still, and will not fall (O Justice!)

  Upon us, for this wicked man?

Face.   Nay, look, sir,   80

  You grieve him now with staying in his sight.

  Good sir, the nobleman will come too, and take you,

  And that may breed a tragedy.

Mam.   I'll go.

Face. Ay, and repent at home, sir. It may be

  For some good penance you may ha' it yet:

  A hundred pound to the box at Bedlam –

Mam.   Yes.

Face. For the restoring such as ha' their wits.

Mam.   I'll do't.

Face. I'll send one to you to receive it.

Mam.   Do.

  Is no projection left?

Face.   All flown, or stinks, sir.

Mam. Will nought be saved that's good for med'cine, think'st

   thou?   90

Face. I cannot tell, sir. There will be, perhaps,

  Something about the scraping of the shards

  Will cure the itch – [*Aside*] though not your itch of mind,

   sir. –

  It shall be saved for you, and sent home. Good sir,

  This way, for fear the lord should meet you.

              [*Exit Mammon.*]

Sub.   Face.

Face. Ay.

Sub.   Is he gone?

Face.   Yes, and as heavily
As all the gold he hoped for were in his blood.
Let us be light, though.

Sub.   Ay, as balls, and bound
And hit our heads against the roof for joy:
There's so much of our care now cast away.   100

Face. Now to our Don.

Sub.   Yes, your young widow by this time,
Is made a Countess, Face. She's been in travail
Of a young heir for you.

Face.   Good, sir.

Sub.   Off with your case,
And greet her kindly, as a bridegroom should,
After these common hazards.

Face.   Very well, sir.
Will you go fetch Don Diego off, the while?

Sub. And fetch him over too, if you'll be pleased, sir.
Would Doll were in her place, to pick his pockets now!

Face. Why, you can do it as well, if you would set to't.
I pray you prove your virtue.

Sub.   For your sake, sir.   110

                                        [*Exeunt.*]

SCENE VI

[*Enter*] SURLY [*and*] DAME PLIANT.

[*Sur.*] Lady, you see into what hands you are fall'n,
    'Mongst what a nest of villains! And how near
    Your honour was t'have catched a certain clap,
    Through your credulity, had I but been
    So punctually forward, as place, time,
    And other circumstance would ha' made a man;
    For you're a handsome woman: would y'were wise, too.
    I am a gentleman, come here disguised
    Only to find the knaveries of this citadel;

And where I might have wronged your honour,
    and have not,   10
I claim some interest in your love. You are,
They say, a widow, rich; and I am a bachelor
Worth nought. Your fortunes may make me a man,
As mine ha' preserved you a woman. Think upon it,
And whether I have deserved you or no.

Pli.   I will, sir.

Sur. And for these household-rogues, let me alone
To treat with them.

[*Enter* SUBTLE.]

Sub.   How doth my noble Diego?
And my dear Madam Countess? Hath the Count
Been courteous, lady? Liberal, and open?
Donzel, methinks you look melancholic   20
After your *coitum*, and scurvy! Truly,
I do not like the dullness of your eye:
It hath a heavy cast, 'tis upsee Dutch,
And says you are a lumpish whoremaster.
Be lighter: I will make your pockets so.

                        He falls to picking of them.

Sur. Will you, Don Bawd, and pickpurse? [*Striking Subtle*]
  How now? Reel you?
Stand up, sir: you shall find since I am so heavy,
I'll gi' you equal weight.

Sub.   Help, murder!

Sur.   No, sir.
There's no such thing intended. A good cart
And a clean whip shall ease you of that fear.   30
I am the Spanish Don that should be cozened,
Do you see? Cozened? Where's your Captain Face,
That parcel-broker, and whole-bawd, all rascal?

[*Enter* FACE.]

Face. How, Surly!

Sur.   O, make your approach, good Captain.

I have found from whence your copper rings and spoons
Come now, wherewith you cheat abroad in taverns.
'Twas here you learned t'anoint your boot with brimstone,
Then rub men's gold on't for a kind of touch,
And say 'twas naught, when you had changed the colour,
That you might ha't for nothing! And this Doctor,   40
Your sooty, smoky-bearded compeer, he
Will close you so much gold in a bolt's-head,
And, on a turn, convey i' the stead another
With sublimed mercury, that shall burst i' the heat,
And fly out all *in fumo*! Then weeps Mammon; [*Exit Face.*]
Then swoons his worship. Or he is the Faustus
That casteth figures and can conjure, cures
Plague, piles and pox by the ephemerides,
And holds intelligence with all the bawds
And midwives of three shires, while you send in,   50
Captain – what, is he gone? – damsels with child,
Wives that are barren, or the waiting-maid
With the green-sickness! Nay, sir, you must tarry
Though he be 'scaped, and answer by the ears, sir.

SCENE VII

[Enter] FACE *[and]* KASTRIL.

[*Face.*] Why, now's the time, if ever you will quarrel
          Well, as they say, and be a true-born child.
          The Doctor and your sister both are abused.
Kas. Where is he? Which is he? He is a slave
          Whate'er he is, and the son of a whore. Are you
          The man, sir, I would know?
Sur.   I should be loath, sir,
          To confess so much.
Kas.   Then you lie i' your throat.
Sur.   How?

Face. A very arrant rogue, sir, and a cheater,
            Employed here by another conjurer
            That does not love the Doctor, and would cross him   10
            If he knew how –
Sur.   Sir, you are abused.
Kas.   You lie,
            And 'tis no matter.
Face.   Well said, sir. He is
            The impudent'st rascal –
Sur.   You are indeed. Will you hear
                me, sir?
Face. By no means. Bid him be gone.
Kas.   Begone, sir, quickly.
Sur. This's strange! Lady, do you inform your brother.
                                [She tries to speak to Kastril.]
Face. There is not such a foist in all the town.
            The Doctor had him presently, and finds yet
            The Spanish Count will come here. *[Aside]* Bear up, Subtle.
Sub. Yes, sir, he must appear within this hour.
Face. And yet this rogue would come in a disguise,   20
            By the temptation of another spirit,
            To trouble our art, though he could not hurt it.
Kas.   Ay,
            I know – *[To Dame Pliant]* Away, you talk like a foolish
                mauther.   *[Exit Dame Pliant.]*
Sur. Sir, all is truth she says.
Face.   Do not believe him, sir:
            He is the lying'st swabber! Come your ways, sir.
Sur. You are valiant, out of company.
Kas.   Yes, how then, sir?

                    [Enter] DRUGGER

Face. Nay, here's an honest fellow, too, that knows him
            And all his tricks. *[Aside to Drugger]* Make good what I
                say, Abel,
            This cheater would ha' cozened thee o' the widow. –
            He owes this honest Drugger here seven pound   30

He has had on him in twopenn'orths of tobacco.

Dru. Yes, sir. And he's damned himself three terms to pay me.

Face. And what does he owe for lotium?

Dru.   Thirty shillings, sir;
And for six syringes.

Sur.   Hydra of villainy!

Face. Nay, sir, you must quarrel him out o' the house.

Kas.   I will.
Sir, if you get not out o' doors, you lie,
And you are a pimp.

Sur.   Why, this is madness, sir,
Not valour in you: I must laugh at this.

Kas. It is my humour: you are a pimp, and a trig,
And an Amadis de Gaul, or a Don Quixote.   40

Dru. Or a Knight o' the Curious Coxcomb. Do you see?

[*Enter*] ANANIAS.

Ana. Peace to the household.

Kas.   I'll keep peace for no man.

Ana. Casting of dollars is concluded lawful.

Kas. Is he the constable?

Sub.   Peace, Ananias.

Face.   No, sir.

Kas. Then you are an otter, and a shad, a whit,
A very tim.

Sur.   You'll hear me, sir?

Kas.   I will not.

Ana. What is the motive?

Sub.   Zeal, in the young gentleman,
Against his Spanish slops –

Ana.   They are profane,
Lewd, superstitious and idolatrous breeches.

Sur. New rascals!

Kas.   Will you be gone, sir?

Ana.   Avoid, Satan!   50
Thou art not of the light. That ruff of pride
About thy neck betrays thee, and is the same

With that which the unclean birds, in seventy-seven,
Were seen to prank it with on divers coasts.
Thou look'st like Antichrist in that lewd hat.

Sur. I must give way.

Kas.   Begone, sir.

Sur.   But I'll take
A course with you –

Ana.   Depart, proud Spanish fiend!

Sur. Captain, and Doctor –

Ana.   Child of perdition!

Kas.   Hence, sir.
                                        [*Exit Surly.*]
Did I not quarrel bravely?

Face.   Yes, indeed, sir.

Kas. Nay, and I give my mind to't, I shall do't.   60

Face. O, you must follow, sir, and threaten him tame.
He'll turn again else.

Kas.   I'll re-turn him then.   [*Exit.*]

Face. Drugger, this rogue prevented us for thee.
We had determined that thou should'st ha' come
In a Spanish suit, and ha' carried her so; and he,
A brokerly slave, goes, puts it on himself.
Hast brought the damask?

Dru.   Yes, sir.

Face.   Thou must borrow
A Spanish suit. Hast thou no credit with the players?

Dru. Yes, sir, did you never see me play the fool?

Face. I know not, Nab; thou shalt, if I can help it.   70
Hieronimo's old cloak, ruff and hat will serve.
I'll tell thee more when thou bring'st 'em.

                    Subtle hath whispered with him [*Ananias*] *this while.*

Ana.   Sir, I know
The Spaniard hates the brethren, and hath spies
Upon their actions; and that this was one,
I make no scruple. But the holy synod
Have been in prayer and meditation for it,
And 'tis revealed no less to them than me,

That casting of money is most lawful.

Sub.   True,
But here I cannot do it; if the house
Should chance to be suspected, all would out,   80
And we be locked up in the Tower for ever,
To make gold there for th'state, never come out;
And then are you defeated.

Ana.   I will tell
This to the elders and the weaker brethren,
That the whole company of the separation
May join in humble prayer again.

Sub.   And fasting.

Ana. Yea, for some fitter place. The peace of mind
Rest with these walls.

Sub.   Thanks, courteous Ananias.

                                              [_Exit Ananias._]

Face. What did he come for?

Sub.   About casting dollars,
Presently, out of hand. And so I told him   90
A Spanish minister came here to spy
Against the faithful –

Face.   I conceive. Come, Subtle,
Thou art so down upon the least disaster!
How would'st th'ha' done, if I had not helped thee out?

Sub. I thank thee, Face, for the angry boy, i' faith.

Face. Who would ha' looked it should ha' been that rascal
Surly? He had dyed his beard, and all. Well, sir,
Here's damask come to make you a suit.

Sub.   Where's Drugger?

Face. He is gone to borrow me a Spanish habit:
I'll be the Count, now.

Sub.   But where's the widow?   100

Face. Within, with my lord's sister: Madam Doll
Is entertaining her.

Sub.   By your favour, Face:
Now she is honest, I will stand again.

Face. You will not offer it?

Sub.   Why?
Face.   Stand to your word,
    Or – here comes Doll. She knows –
Sub.   You're tyrannous still.

                [*Enter*] DOLL.

Face. Strict for my right. How now, Doll? Hast told her
    The Spanish Count will come?
Doll.   Yes, but another is come
    You little looked for!
Face.   Who's that?
Doll.   Your master,
    The master of the house.
Sub.   How, Doll!
Face.   She lies.
    This is some trick. Come, leave your quiblins,
      Dorothy.   110
Doll. Look out, and see.
Sub.   Art thou in earnest?
Doll.   'Slight,
    Forty o' the neighbours are about him, talking.
Face. [*Looking out*] 'Tis he, by this good day.
Doll.   'Twill prove ill
    day
    For some on us.
Face.   We are undone, and taken.
Doll. Lost, I am afraid.
Sub.   You said he would not come
    While there died one a week within the liberties.
Face. No: 'twas within the walls.
Sub.   Was't so? Cry you mercy:
    I thought the liberties. What shall we do now, Face?
Face. Be silent: not a word, if he call or knock.
    I'll into mine old shape again and meet him,   120
    Of Jeremy the butler. I' the meantime,
    Do you two pack up all the goods and purchase
    That we can carry i' the two trunks. I'll keep him

Off for today, if I cannot longer, and then
At night I'll ship you both away to Ratcliff,
Where we'll meet tomorrow, and there we'll share.
Let Mammon's brass and pewter keep the cellar;
We'll have another time for that. But, Doll,
'Pray thee go heat a little water quickly:
Subtle must shave me. All my Captain's beard   130
Must off, to make me appear smooth Jeremy.
You'll do't?

Sub.   Yes, I'll shave you as well as I can.

Face. And not cut my throat, but trim me?

Sub.   You shall see, sir.

                                        [*Exeunt.*]

ACT V

SCENE I

[*Enter*] LOVEWIT [*and*] Neighbours.

[*Lov.*] Has there been such resort, say you?
Nei. 1.   Daily, sir.
Nei. 2. And nightly, too.
Nei. 3.   Ay, some as brave as lords.
Nei. 4. Ladies and gentlewomen.
Nei. 5.   Citizen's wives.
Nei. 1. And knights.
Nei. 6.   In coaches.
Nei. 2.   Yes, and oyster-women.
Nei. 1. Beside other gallants.
Nei. 3.   Sailors' wives.
Nei. 4.   Tobacco-men.
Nei. 5. Another Pimlico!
Lov.   What should my knave advance,
    To draw this company? He hung out no banners
    Of a strange calf with five legs to be seen?
    Or a huge lobster with six claws?
Nei. 6.   No, sir.
Nei. 3. We had gone in then, sir.
Lov.   He has no gift   10
    Of teaching i' the nose that e'er I knew of!
    You saw no bills set up, that promised cure
    Of agues or the toothache?
Nei. 2.   No such thing, sir.
Lov. Nor heard a drum struck for baboons or puppets?

Nei. 5. Neither, sir.

Lov.   What device should he bring forth now?
I love a teeming wit as I love my nourishment.
'Pray God he ha' not kept such open house
That he hath sold my hangings and my bedding;
I left him nothing else. If he have eat 'em,
A plague o' the moth, say I. Sure he has got   20
Some bawdy pictures, to call all this ging:
The Friar and the Nun, or the new motion
Of the Knight's courser covering the Parson's mare;
The boy of six years old with the great thing;
Or't may be he has the fleas that run at tilt
Upon a table, or some dog to dance?
When saw you him?

Nei. 1.   Who, sir, Jeremy?
Nei. 2.   Jeremy butler?
We saw him not this month.

Lov.   How!
Nei. 4.   Not these five weeks,
     sir.

Nei. 1. These six weeks, at the least.

Lov.   Y'amaze me, neighbours!

Nei. 5. Sure, if your worship know not where he is,   30
He's slipped away.

Nei. 6.   'Pray God he be not made away!

Lov. Ha? It's no time to question, then.   *He knocks.*

Nei. 6.   About
Some three weeks since, I heard a doleful cry,
As I sat up a-mending my wife's stockings.

Lov. This's strange, that none will answer! Didst thou hear
A cry, sayst thou?

Nei. 6.   Yes, sir, like unto a man
That had been strangled an hour, and could not speak.

Nei. 2. I heard it too, just this day three weeks, at two o'clock
Next morning.

Lov.   These be miracles, or you make 'em so!
A man an hour strangled, and could not speak,   40

And both you heard him cry?
Nei. 3.   Yes, downward, sir.
Lov. Thou art a wise fellow; give me thy hand, I pray thee.
    What trade art thou on?
Nei. 3.   A smith, and't please your worship.
Lov. A smith? Then lend me thy help to get this door open.
Nei. 3. That I will presently, sir, but fetch my tools –   [*Exit.*]
Nei. 1. Sir, best to knock again afore you break it.

SCENE II

[*Enter*] FACE.

[*Lov.*] I will.
Face.   What mean you, sir?
Nei. 1, 2, 4.   O, here's Jeremy!
Face. Good sir, come from the door.
Lov.   Why! What's the matter?
Face. Yet farther, you are too near, yet.
Lov.   I' the name of wonder!
    What means the fellow?
Face.   The house, sir, has been visited.
Lov. What? With the plague? Stand thou then farther.
Face.   No, sir,
    I had it not.
Lov.   Who had it then? I left
    None else but thee i' the house!
Face.   Yes, sir. My fellow
    The cat that kept the butt'ry had it on her
    A week before I spied it, but I got her
    Conveyed away i' the night. And so I shut   10
    The house up for a month –
Lov.   How!
Face.   Purposing then, sir,
    T'have burnt rose-vinegar, treacle and tar,
    And ha' made it sweet, and you should ne'er ha' known it;

Because I knew the news would but afflict you, sir.
Lov. Breathe less, and farther off. Why, this is stranger!
    The neighbours tell me all, here, that the doors
    Have still been open –
Face.   How, sir!
Lov.   Gallants, men and women,
    And of all sorts, tag-rag, been seen to flock here
    In threaves, these ten weeks, as to a second Hogsden
    In days of Pimlico and Eye-bright!
Face.   Sir,   20
    Their wisdoms will not say so!
Lov.   Today they speak
    Of coaches and gallants; one in a French hood
    Went in, they tell me; and another was seen
    In a velvet gown at the window! Divers more
    Pass in and out!
Face.   They did pass through the doors then,
    Or walls, I assure their eyesights and their spectacles;
    For here, sir, are the keys, and here have been
    In this my pocket now above twenty days!
    And for before, I kept the fort alone there.
    But that 'tis yet not deep i' the afternoon,   30
    I should believe my neighbours had seen double
    Through the black-pot, and made these apparitions!
    For, on my faith to your worship, for these three weeks
    And upwards, the door has not been opened.
Lov.   Strange!
Nei. 1. Good faith, I think I saw a coach!
Nei. 2.   And I too,
    I'd ha' been sworn!
Lov.   Do you but think it now?
    And but one coach?
Nei. 4.   We cannot tell, sir: Jeremy
    Is a very honest fellow.
Face.   Did you see me at all?
Nei. 1. No, that we are sure on.
Nei. 2.   I'll be sworn o' that.

Lov. Fine rogues, to have your testimonies built on!   40

[*Enter* Neighbour 3.]

Nei. 3. Is Jeremy come?
Nei. 1.   O, yes, you may leave your tools;
    We were deceived, he says.
Nei. 2.   He has had the keys,
    And the door has been shut these three weeks.
Nei. 3.   Like enough.
Lov. Peace, and get hence, you changelings.
Face. [*Aside, seeing Mammon and Surly*]   Surly come!
    And Mammon made acquainted? They'll tell all.
    How shall I beat them off? What shall I do?
    Nothing's more wretched than a guilty conscience.

SCENE III

[*Enter*] SURLY [*and*] MAMMON.

[*Sur.*] No, sir, he was a great physician. This,
    It was no bawdy-house, but a mere chancel.
    You knew the lord and his sister.
Mam.   Nay, good Surly –
Sur. The happy word, 'Be rich' –
Mam.   Play not the tyrant –
Sur. Should be today pronounced to all your friends.
    And where be your andirons now? And your brass pots?
    That should ha' been golden flagons and great wedges?
Mam. Let me but breathe. What! They ha' shut their doors,
    Methinks!   *Mammon and Surly knock.*
Sur.   Ay, now 'tis holiday with them.
Mam.   Rogues,
    Cozeners, impostors, bawds!
Face.   What mean you, sir?   10
Mam. To enter if we can.
Face.   Another man's house?

    Here is the owner, sir. Turn you to him,
    And speak your business.
Mam.   Are you, sir, the owner?
Lov. Yes, sir.
Mam.   And are those knaves within your cheaters?
Lov. What knaves? What cheaters?
Mam.   Subtle and his Lungs.
Face. The gentleman is distracted, sir! No lungs
    Nor lights ha' been seen here these three weeks, sir,
    Within these doors, upon my word!
Sur.   Your word,
    Groom arrogant!
Face.   Yes, sir, I am the housekeeper,
    And know the keys ha' not been out o' my hands.   20
Sur. This's a new Face!
Face.   You do mistake the house, sir!
    What sign was't at?
Sur.   You rascal! This is one
    O' the confederacy. Come, let's get officers,
    And force the door.
Lov.   'Pray you stay, gentlemen.
Sur. No, sir, we'll come with warrant.
Mam.   Ay, and then
    We shall ha' your doors open.
                   [Exeunt Mammon and Surly.]
Lov.   What means this?
Face. I cannot tell, sir!
Nei. 1.   These are two o' the gallants
    That we do think we saw.
Face.   Two o' the fools!
    You talk as idly as they. Good faith, sir,
    I think the moon has crazed 'em all!

                [Enter KASTRIL.*]*

[Aside]   O me,   30
    The angry boy come too? He'll make a noise,
    And ne'er away till he have betrayed us all.   *Kastril knocks.*

Kas. What! Rogues, bawds, slaves, you'll open the door, anon!
     Punk, cockatrice, my suster! By this light
     I'll fetch the marshal to you. You are a whore
     To keep your castle –
Face.   Who would you speak with, sir?
Kas. The bawdy Doctor, and the cozening Captain,
     And Puss my suster.
Lov.   This is something, sure!
Face. Upon my trust, the doors were never open, sir.
Kas. I have heard all their tricks told me twice over   40
     By the fat knight and the lean gentleman.

                [*Enter* ANANIAS *and* TRIBULATION.]

Lov. Here comes another.
Face. [*Aside*]   Ananias too?
     And his pastor?   *They beat, too, at the door.*
Tri.   The doors are shut against us.
Ana. Come forth, you seed of sulphur, sons of fire!
     Your stench, it is broke forth: abomination
     Is in the house.
Kas.   Ay, my suster's there.
Ana.   The place,
     It is become a cage of unclean birds.
Kas. Yes, I will fetch the scavenger and the constable.
Tri. You shall do well.
Ana.   We'll join to weed them out.
Kas. You will not come then? Punk device, my suster!   50
Ana. Call her not sister. She is a harlot, verily.
Kas. I'll raise the street.
Lov.   Good gentlemen, a word.
Ana. Satan, avoid, and hinder not our zeal!
Lov. The world's turned Bedlam.
Face.   These are all broke loose
     Out of St Kather'ne's, where they use to keep
     The better sort of mad-folks.
Nei. 1.   All these persons
     We saw go in and out here.

Nei. 2.   Yes, indeed, sir.

Nei. 3. These were the parties.

Face.   Peace, you drunkards. Sir,
    I wonder at it! Please you to give me leave
    To touch the door; I'll try and the lock be changed.   60

Lov. It mazes me!

Face.   Good faith, sir, I believe
    There's no such thing. 'Tis all *deceptio visus*.
    [*Aside*] Would I could get him away.

                          Dapper cries out within.

Dap.   Master Captain,
    Master Doctor!

Lov. Who's that?

Face. [*Aside*]   Our clerk within, that I forgot! – I know not,
     sir.

Dap. [*Within*] For God's sake, when will her Grace be at
    leisure?

Face.   Ha!
    Illusions, some spirit o' the air. [*Aside*] His gag is melted,
    And now he sets out the throat.

Dap. [*Within*]   I am almost stifled –

Face. [*Aside*] Would you were altogether.

Lov.   'Tis i' the house.
    Ha! List.

Face.   Believe it, sir, i' the air!

Lov.   Peace, you –

Dap. [*Within*] Mine aunt's Grace does not use me well.

Sub. [*Within*]   You
    fool,   70
    Peace, you'll mar all.

Face. [*To Subtle within*]   Or you will else, you rogue.

Lov. O, is it so? Then you converse with spirits!
    Come, sir. No more o' your tricks, good Jeremy;
    The truth, the shortest way.

Face.   Dismiss this rabble, sir.
    [*Aside*] What shall I do? I am catched.

Lov.   Good neighbours,

I thank you all. You may depart.   [*Exeunt Neighbours.*]
                                        Come, sir,
You know that I am an indulgent master;
And therefore conceal nothing. What's your med'cine
To draw so many several sorts of wild-fowl?
Face. Sir, you were wont to affect mirth and wit –   80
     But here's no place to talk on't i' the street.
     Give me but leave to make the best of my fortune,
     And only pardon me th'abuse of your house:
     It's all I beg. I'll help you to a widow
     In recompense, that you shall gi' me thanks for,
     Will make you seven years younger, and a rich one.
     'Tis but your putting on a Spanish cloak;
     I have her within. You need not fear the house,
     It was not visited.
Lov.   But by me, who came
     Sooner than you expected.
Face.   It is true, sir.   90
     'Pray you forgive me.
Lov.   Well, let's see your widow.
                                        [*Exeunt.*]

SCENE IV

[*Enter*] SUBTLE [*and*] DAPPER.

[*Sub.*] How! Ha' you eaten your gag?
Dap.   Yes faith, it crumbled
     Away i' my mouth.
Sub.   You ha' spoiled all, then.
Dap.   No,
     I hope my aunt of Fairy will forgive me.
Sub. Your aunt's a gracious lady; but in troth
     You were to blame.
Dap.   The fume did overcome me,
     And I did do't to stay my stomach. 'Pray you

So satisfy her Grace. Here comes the Captain.

[*Enter* FACE.]

Face. How now? Is his mouth down?
Sub.   Ay! He has spoken!
Face. [*To Subtle*] A pox, I heard him, and you too. –
      [*Aloud*] He's undone, then. –
      [*Face and Subtle talk aside.*] I have been fain to say the
         house is haunted   10
      With spirits, to keep churl back.
Sub.   And hast thou done it?
Face. Sure, for this night.
Sub.   Why, then triumph, and sing
      Of Face so famous, the precious king
      Of present wits!
Face.   Did you not hear the coil
      About the door?
Sub.   Yes, and I dwindled with it.
Face. [*Aloud*] Show him his aunt, and let him be dispatched:
      I'll send her to you.   [*Exit.*]
Sub.   Well, sir, your aunt her Grace
      Will give you audience presently, on my suit
      And the Captain's word that you did not eat your gag
      In any contempt of her Highness.
Dap.   Not I, in troth, sir.   20

[*Enter*] DOLL *like the Queen of Fairy.*

Sub. Here she is come. Down o' your knees, and wriggle:
      She has a stately presence. Good. Yet nearer,
      And bid, 'God save you!'
Dap.   Madam.
Sub.   And your aunt.
Dap. And my most gracious aunt, God save your Grace.
Doll. Nephew, we thought to have been angry with you,
      But that sweet face of yours hath turned the tide,
      And made it flow with joy, that ebbed of love.
      Arise, and touch our velvet gown.

Sub.   The skirts,
   And kiss 'em. So.

Doll.   Let me now stroke that head.
   Much, nephew, shalt thou win; much shalt thou spend;   30
   Much shalt thou give away; much shalt thou lend.

Sub. [*Aside*] Ay, much, indeed. – Why do you not thank her
   Grace?

Dap. I cannot speak, for joy.

Sub.   See, the kind wretch!
   Your Grace's kinsman right.

Doll.   Give me the bird.
   Here is your fly in a purse, about your neck, cousin;
   Wear it, and feed it about this day se'night,
   On your right wrist –

Sub.   Open a vein with a pin,
   And let it suck but once a week; till then,
   You must not look on't.

Doll.   No. And, kinsman,
   Bear yourself worthy of the blood you come on.   40

Sub. Her Grace would ha' you eat no more Woolsack pies,
   Nor Dagger frumety.

Doll.   Nor break his fast
   In Heaven and Hell.

Sub.   She's with you everywhere!
   Nor play with costermongers at mumchance, tray-trip,
   God-make-you-rich (when as your aunt has done it), but
      keep
   The gallant'st company, and the best games –

Dap.   Yes, sir.

Sub. Gleek and primero; and what you get, be true to us.

Dap. By this hand, I will.

Sub.   You may bring's a thousand pound
   Before tomorrow night, if but three thousand
   Be stirring, and you will.

Dap.   I swear I will, then.   50

Sub. Your fly will learn you all games.

Face. [*Within*]   Ha' you done there?

Sub. Your Grace will command him no more duties?
Doll.   No,
    But come and see me often. I may chance
    To leave him three or four hundred chests of treasure,
    And some twelve thousand acres of Fairyland,
    If he game well and comely with good gamesters.
Sub. There's a kind aunt! Kiss her departing part.
    But you must sell your forty mark a year now.
Dap. Ay, sir, I mean.
Sub.   Or, gi't away: pox on't.
Dap. I'll gi't mine aunt. I'll go and fetch the writings.   60
 Sub. 'Tis well, away.   [*Exit Dapper.*]

[Enter FACE.]

Face.   Where's Subtle?
Sub.   Here. What news?
Face. Drugger is at the door. Go take his suit,
    And bid him fetch a parson presently;
    Say he shall marry the widow. Thou shalt spend
    A hundred pound by the service!   [*Exit Subtle.*]
               Now, Queen Doll,
    Ha' you packed up all?
Doll.   Yes.
Face.   And how do you like
    The Lady Pliant?
Doll.   A good, dull innocent.

[Enter SUBTLE.]

Sub. Here's your Hieronimo's cloak and hat.
Face.   Give me 'em.
Sub. And the ruff too?
Face.   Yes, I'll come to you presently.   [*Exit.*]
Sub. Now he is gone about his project, Doll,   70
    I told you of, for the widow.
Doll.   'Tis direct
    Against our articles.
Sub.   Well, we'll fit him, wench.

Hast thou gulled her of her jewels or her bracelets?

Doll. No, but I will do't.

Sub.   Soon at night, my Dolly,
When we are shipped, and all our goods aboard,
Eastward for Ratcliff, we will turn our course
To Brainford, westward, if thou sayst the word,
And take our leaves of this o'erweening rascal,
This peremptory Face.

Doll.   Content: I'm weary of him.

Sub. Thou'st cause, when the slave will run a-wiving, Doll,   80
Against the instrument that was drawn between us.

Doll. I'll pluck his bird as bare as I can.

Sub.   Yes, tell her
She must by any means address some present
To th'cunning man, make him amends for wronging
His art with her suspicion; send a ring,
Or chain of pearl; she will be tortured else
Extremely in her sleep, say, and ha' strange things
Come to her. Wilt thou?

Doll.   Yes.

Sub.   My fine flitter-mouse,
My bird o' the night; we'll tickle it at the Pigeons
When we have all, and may unlock the trunks,   90
And say, 'This's mine and thine, and thine, and mine' –

                              They kiss.

[*Enter* FACE.]

Face. What now, a-billing?

Sub.   Yes, a little exalted
In the good passage of our stock-affairs.

Face. Drugger has brought his parson; take him in, Subtle,
And send Nab back again to wash his face.

Sub. I will; and shave himself?

Face.   If you can get him. [*Exit Subtle.*]

Doll. You are hot upon it, Face, whate'er it is!

Face. A trick that Doll shall spend ten pound a month by.

[*Enter* SUBTLE.]

     Is he gone?
Sub.   The chaplain waits you i' the hall, sir.
Face. I'll go bestow him.   [*Exit.*]
Doll.   He'll now marry her instantly.   100
Sub. He cannot yet: he is not ready. Dear Doll,
    Cozen her of all thou canst. To deceive him
    Is no deceit, but justice, that would break
    Such an inextricable tie as ours was.
Doll. Let me alone to fit him.

                [*Enter* FACE.]

Face.   Come, my venturers,
    You ha' packed up all? Where be the trunks? Bring forth.
Sub. Here.
Face.   Let's see 'em. Where's the money?
Sub.   Here,
    In this.
Face.   Mammon's ten pound; eight score before.
    The brethren's money, this. Drugger's, and Dapper's.
    What paper's that?
Doll.   The jewel of the waiting-maid's,   110
    That stole it from her lady, to know certain –
Face. If she should have precedence of her mistress?
Doll.   Yes.
Face. What box is that?
Sub.   The fishwives' rings, I think,
    And th'alewives' single money. Is't not, Doll?
Doll. Yes, and the whistle that the sailor's wife
    Brought you, to know and her husband were with Ward.
Face. We'll wet it tomorrow, and our silver beakers
    And tavern cups. Where be the French petticoats
    And girdles, and hangers?
Sub.   Here, i' the trunk,
    And the bolts of lawn.
Face.   Is Drugger's damask there?   120
    And the tobacco?

Sub.   Yes.

Face.   Give me the keys.

Doll. Why you the keys?

Sub.   No matter, Doll, because
  We shall not open 'em before he comes.

Face. 'Tis true, you shall not open them, indeed,
  Nor have 'em forth. Do you see? Not forth, Doll.

Doll.   No?

Face. No, my smock-rampant. The right is, my master
  Knows all, has pardoned me, and he will keep 'em.
  Doctor, 'tis true – you look – for all your figures;
  I sent for him indeed. Wherefore, good partners,
  Both he and she, be satisfied; for here   130
  Determines the indenture tripartite
  'Twixt Subtle, Doll and Face. All I can do
  Is to help you over the wall o' the back-side,
  Or lend you a sheet to save your velvet gown, Doll.
  Here will be officers presently; bethink you
  Of some course suddenly to 'scape the dock,
  For thither you'll come else.   *Some knock.*
                        Hark you, thunder.

Sub. You are a precious fiend!

Off. [*Within*]   Open the door.

Face. Doll, I am sorry for thee, i' faith. But hear'st thou?
  It shall go hard but I will place thee somewhere: 140
  Thou shalt ha' my letter to Mistress Amo –

Doll.   Hang you –

Face. Or Madam Caesarean.

Doll.   Pox upon you, rogue,
  Would I had but time to beat thee.

Face.   Subtle,
  Let's know where you set up next; I'll send you
  A customer now and then, for old acquaintance:
  What new course ha' you?

Sub.   Rogue, I'll hang myself
  That I may walk a greater devil than thou,
  And haunt thee i' the flock-bed and the buttery. [*Exeunt.*]

SCENE V

[*Enter*] LOVEWIT [*in the Spanish costume with the* Parson].

[*Lov.*] What do you mean, my masters?
Mam. [*Within*]   Open your door,
  Cheaters, bawds, conjurers!
Off. [*Within.*]   Or we'll break it open.
Lov. What warrant have you?
Off. [*Within*]   Warrant enough, sir, doubt not,
  If you'll not open it.
Lov.   Is there an officer there?
Off. [*Within*] Yes, two or three for failing.
Lov.   Have but patience,
  And I will open it straight.

[*Enter*] FACE.

Face.   Sir, ha' you done?
  Is it a marriage? Perfect?
Lov.   Yes, my brain.
Face. Off with your ruff and cloak then: be yourself, sir.
Sur. [*Within*] Down with the door.
Kas. [*Within*]   'Slight, ding it open.
Lov.   Hold,
  Hold, gentlemen; what means this violence?   10

[*Enter*] MAMMON [*and*] SURLY.

Mam. Where is this collier?
Sur.   And my Captain Face?
Mam. These day-owls –
Sur.   That are birding in men's purses.

[*Enter*] KASTRIL.

Mam. Madam Suppository.
Kas.   Doxy, my suster.

[*Enter*] ANANIAS [*and*] TRIBULATION.

Ana.   Locusts

Of the foul pit –

Tri.   Profane as Bel, and the Dragon –

Ana. Worse than the grasshoppers or the lice of Egypt.

[*Enter*] Officers.

Lov. Good gentlemen, hear me. Are you officers,
And cannot stay this violence?

Off. 1.   Keep the peace!

Lov. Gentlemen, what is the matter? Whom do you seek?

Mam. The chemical cozener.

Sur.   And the Captain pander.

Kas. The nun my suster.

Mam.   Madam Rabbi.

Ana.   Scorpions   20
And caterpillars.

Lov.   Fewer at once, I pray you.

Off. 1. One after another, gentlemen, I charge you,
By virtue of my staff –

Ana.   They are the vessels
Of pride, lust, and the cart.

Lov.   Good zeal, lie still
A little while.

Tri.   Peace, Deacon Ananias.

Lov. The house is mine here, and the doors are open:
If there be any such persons as you seek for,
Use your authority, search on o' God's name.
I am but newly come to town, and finding
This tumult 'bout my door, to tell you true,   30
It somewhat mazed me; till my man here, fearing
My more displeasure, told me he had done
Somewhat an insolent part, let out my house
(Belike, presuming on my known aversion
From any air o' the town while there was sickness)
To a Doctor and a Captain; who, what they are,
Or where they be, he knows not.

Mam.   Are they gone?

Lov. You may go in and search, sir.

   They [*Tribulation, Ananias, Mammon*] *enter* [*the house*].

       Here I find
 The empty walls worse than I left 'em, smoked;
 A few cracked pots and glasses, and a furnace;   40
 The ceiling filled with poesies of the candle,
 And madam with a dildo writ o' the walls.
 Only one gentlewoman I met here,
 That is within, that said she was a widow –

Kas. Ay, that's my suster. I'll go thump her. Where is she?
                 [*Exit.*]

Lov. And should ha' married a Spanish Count, but he,
 When he came to't, neglected her so grossly
 That I, a widower, am gone through with her.

Sur. How! Have I lost her then?

Lov.   Were you the Don, Sir?
 Good faith, now, she does blame y'extremely, and
  says   50
 You swore, and told her you had ta'en the pains
 To dye your beard, and umber o'er your face,
 Borrowed a suit and ruff, all for her love;
 And then did nothing. What an oversight,
 And want of putting forward, sir, was this!
 Well fare an old harquebusier yet,
 Could prime his powder, and give fire, and hit,
 All in a twinkling.

      MAMMON *comes forth.*

Mam.   The whole nest are fled!

Lov. What sort of birds were they?

Mam.   A kind of choughs
 Or thievish daws, sir, that have picked my purse 60
 Of eight-score and ten pounds within these five weeks,
 Beside my first materials and my goods
 That lie i' the cellar, which I am glad they ha' left.
 I may have home yet.

Lov.   Think you so, sir?

Mam.   Ay.

Lov. By order of law, sir, but not otherwise.

Mam. Not mine own stuff?

Lov.   Sir, I can take no knowledge
That they are yours, but by public means.
If you can bring certificate that you were gulled of 'em,
Or any formal writ out of a court
That you did cozen yourself, I will not hold them.   70

Mam. I'll rather lose 'em.

Lov.   That you shall not, sir,
By me, in troth. Upon these terms they are yours.
What should they ha' been, sir, turned into gold, all?

Mam.   No.
I cannot tell. It may be they should. What then?

Lov. What a great loss in hope have you sustained!

Mam. Not I; the commonwealth has.

Face.   Ay, he would ha' built
The city new, and made a ditch about it
Of silver, should have run with cream from Hogsden,
That every Sunday in Moorfields, the younkers,
And tits, and tomboys should have fed on, *gratis*.   80

Mam. I will go mount a turnip-cart, and preach
The end o' the world within these two months. Surly,
What! In a dream?

Sur.   Must I needs cheat myself
With that same foolish vice of honesty!
Come let us go, and hearken out the rogues.
That Face I'll mark for mine, if e'er I meet him.

Face. If I can hear of him, sir, I'll bring you word
Unto your lodging; for, in troth, they were strangers
To me. I thought 'em honest as myself, sir.

                              [*Exeunt Mammon and Surly.*]

            They [ANANIAS *and* TRIBULATION] *come forth.*

Tri. 'Tis well, the saints shall not lose all yet. Go   90
And get some carts –

Lov.   For what, my zealous friends?

Ana. To bear away the portion of the righteous
    Out of this den of thieves.

Lov.   What is that portion?

Ana. The goods, sometime the orphans', that the brethren
    Bought with their silver pence.

Lov.   What, those i' the cellar
    The knight Sir Mammon claims?

Ana.   I do defy
    The wicked Mammon; so do all the brethren,
    Thou profane man. I ask thee, with what conscience
    Thou canst advance that idol against us,
    That have the seal? Were not the shillings numbered   100
    That made the pounds? Were not the pounds told out
    Upon the second day of the fourth week,
    In the eighth month, upon the table dormant,
    The year of the last patience of the saints,
    Six hundred and ten?

Lov.   Mine earnest vehement botcher,
    And Deacon also, I cannot dispute with you,
    But if you get you not away the sooner,
    I shall confute you with a cudgel.

Ana.   Sir.

Tri. Be patient, Ananias.

Ana.   I am strong,
    And will stand up, well girt, against an host   110
    That threaten Gad in exile.

Lov.   I shall send you
    To Amsterdam, to your cellar.

Ana.   I will pray there
    Against thy house: may dogs defile thy walls,
    And wasps and hornets breed beneath thy roof;
    This seat of falsehood, and this cave of coz'nage.

Lov. Another too?

           DRUGGER *enters and he beats him away.*

Dru.   Not I, sir, I am no brother.

Lov. Away you Harry Nicholas, do you talk?

Face. No, this was Abel Drugger. (*To the Parson*) Good sir, go

And satisfy him; tell him all is done:
He stayed too long a-washing of his face.   120
The Doctor, he shall hear of him at Westchester,
And of the Captain, tell him, at Yarmouth, or
Some good port-town else, lying for a wind. [*Exit Parson.*]
If you get off the angry child now, sir –

[*Enter* KASTRIL *speaking*] *to his sister.*

Kas. Come on, you ewe, you have matched most sweetly, ha'
    you not?
  Did not I say I would never ha' you tupped
  But by a dubbed boy, to make you a lady-tom?
  'Slight, you are a mammet! O, I could touse you now.
  Death, mun' you marry with a pox?
Lov.   You lie, boy!
  As sound as you, and I am aforehand with you.
Kas.   Anon?   130
Lov. Come, will you quarrel? I will feize you, sirrah.
  Why do you not buckle to your tools?
Kas.   God's light!
  This is a fine old boy as e'er I saw!
Lov. What, do you change your copy now? Proceed:
  Here stands my dove; stoop at her if you dare.
Kas. 'Slight, I must love him! I cannot choose, i' faith,
  And I should be hanged for't! Suster, I protest
  I honour thee for this match.
Lov.   O, do you so, sir?
Kas. Yes, and thou canst take tobacco and drink, old boy,
  I'll give her five hundred pound more to her marriage   140
  Than her own state.
Lov.   Fill a pipe-full, Jeremy.
Face. Yes, but go in and take it, sir.
Lov.   We will.
  I will be ruled by thee in anything, Jeremy.
Kas. 'Slight, thou art not hide-bound! Thou art a Jovy boy!
  Come, let's in, I pray thee, and take our whiffs.
Lov. Whiff in with your sister, brother boy.
                 [*Exeunt Kastril and Dame Pliant.*]

[*To the audience*]   That master
That had received such happiness by a servant,
In such a widow, and with so much wealth,
Were very ungrateful if he would not be
A little indulgent to that servant's wit,   150
And help his fortune, though with some small strain
Of his own candour. Therefore, gentlemen,
And kind spectators, if I have outstripped
An old man's gravity, or strict canon, think
What a young wife and a good brain may do:
Stretch age's truth sometimes, and crack it too. –
Speak for thyself, knave.

Face.   So I will, sir.
[*To the audience*]   Gentlemen,
My part a little fell in this last scene,
Yet 'twas decorum. And though I am clean
Got off from Subtle, Surly, Mammon, Doll,   160
Hot Ananias, Dapper, Drugger, all
With whom I traded, yet I put myself
On you, that are my country; and this pelf
Which I have got, if you do quit me, rests
To feast you often, and invite new guests.   [*Exeunt.*]

THE END

This Comedy was first
acted in the year
1610.

By the King's Majesty's
SERVANTS.

The principal Comedians were

RIC[HARD] BURBAGE   JOH[N] HEMINGES
JOH[N] LOWIN   WILL[IAM] OSTLER
HEN[RY] CONDELL   JOH[N] UNDERWOOD
ALEX[ANDER] COOKE   NIC[HOLAS] TOOLEY
ROB[ERT] ARMIN   WILL[IAM] ECCLESTON

With the allowance of the Master of REVELS.

Critical commentary

CONSTRUCTION

The construction of *The Alchemist* reveals the craftsmanship that Ben Johnson valued so highly. Coleridge thought the plot 'perfect', and Dryden remarked on the great variety of character and incident that the play manages to contain without compromising its unity of design.[1] In accordance with neo-classical principles, Jonson observes the 'unities' of place, time and action. The unities were a distillation of the ancient world's dramatic criticism and practice, and were usually defended on the grounds that to extend a play's action beyond one location and its actual playing time in the theatre, and to complicate it with diversions and underplots, offended against rational canons of verisimilitude and credibility. Although the mainstream of Renaissance drama largely ignored these rules, despite the strictures of neo-classical critics such as Sidney and Jonson, the observance of the unities in *The Alchemist* is no mere pedantry, but imaginative and theatrically effective. Jonson aims to give to his comedy of London life the aesthetic *gravitas* of classical tradition, yet he also contrives an unfailing spontaneity in the action.

The open stage of the Jacobean playhouse becomes one room of Lovewit's house for almost the entire play. Of the two entrances that in all probability stood at either side of the stage's rear wall, one will lead to the street, the other to cellar, laboratory, bedchamber and garden. The few scenes set in the street outside (Mammon and Surly, II.i; the Anabaptists, III.i; Lovewit, V.i–iii) serve, together with various knockings at the door and clamourings of voices off, to emphasize the intensity and confinement of the place where the rogues create and sustain their special world. The effect on the audience is perhaps to make them identify with the kings of this little space and applaud the illusions they conjure within it, and their defence of it against the world. But there may be other feelings too: a sense of claustrophobia and anxiety attending the manipulations of personality and identity that occur there as the victims pass from the real world of the street into the distorting mirror of the swindlers' den.

The action is confined to one day, in keeping with neoclassical decorum, and the time-scheme is carefully worked out, beginning at the coming of full daylight and ending in the late afternoon. But far more important for the audience, who will hardly notice the exact duration of the illusion of time in the theatre, is the rhythm of the action. Knocks at the door, entrances and exits are our means of marking the passage of time, and through them Jonson contrives a gathering speed that reaches its peak by the end of Act IV. Finally mimetic time is wound down to the real time of the theatrical present in the speeches to the audience by Lovewit and Face at the end. That the passage of time in the play is a complex experience is well illustrated by the case of Dapper, who, having entered the house without a watch, becomes suspended in the privy's unpleasant limbo for much of Acts IV and V. His enchanting in V.iv is invested with an appropriate timelessness, despite the frenetic activity that surrounds it.

The action itself is unified but rather more elaborate than that of the classical comedies that were Jonson's models. There are seven separate plot-lines, each concerned with gulling, each at a different stage of development, and all brilliantly organized into an action of growing complexity. The control of the plot is in the hands of the three rogues, and dramatic tension is sustained as it constantly threatens to slip from their grasp. An internal threat to the rogues' confederacy lends additional edge to this tension, as the quarrel between Face and Subtle that begins the play flares up again in the disagreement over who will marry Pliant, and culminates in Face's betrayal of his colleagues to Lovewit. Each new shift demanded by an unforeseen event, the constant necessity of keeping all the gulls in ignorance of each other, the complications caused by the intervention of Surly, and then of Lovewit; all these challenge their quickness of wit, and beget a curious mixture of professional rivalry and mutual admiration within the 'venture tripartite' (e.g. IV.iii.50 ff.; IV.vii.92 ff.), as well as involuntary approval from the audience.

The identification between audience and rogues sets up other tensions. Not only are we drawn into a sympathetic relationship with criminals that contradicts all our most respectable feelings, but we may also begin to wonder how far the activities of the dramatist himself coincide with those of the dishonest characters who control the action from within the play. The sustaining of illusion is crucial to both. It is here, as we encounter Jonson's exploitation of the unsettling pleasures (and anxieties) of farce, that simple notions about the 'image of the times' presented by the play must perish, and the critical debate about the morality of comedy begins.

The construction of the play owes much to the Roman New Comedy (especially Plautus), which was essentially a drama of witty but amoral intrigue. But, in using the alchemical swindle as his organizing metaphor to tie the various characters together, Jonson reveals an indebtedness to the 'Old Comedy' of Aristophanes (c. 448–380 BC), in which the dishonest schemes of imaginative rogues become the satiric touchstones of human folly. The unity of the play derives not primarily from the mechanical organization of the complex plot, but from the metaphor that stands at its centre. The processes of alchemy become the very dynamics of the action. The play has a unity created not so much by the rather limited concepts of realism in neo-classical theory as by a comic vision of men united in folly and mutual incomprehension.

CHARACTER

Jonson's comic characters are often seen as schematic simplifications of human beings, essentially static and unchangeable. Such terms generally convey the disapproval, or at least the unease, of the critic, and the comparison with Shakespeare that has bedevilled and distorted discussion of Jonson has added its own negative force to this kind of judgement. It became commonplace, as the often unthinking idolatry of Shakespeare grew during the eighteenth century, to denigrate Jonson as a coarse and narrow pedant in order to praise the 'infinite variety' of the Swan of Avon. Hazlitt's use of Jonson as a whipping boy in this regard in his *Lectures on the English Comic Writers* (1819) represents the disgraceful nadir of this tradition, and sets the tone for the neglect of Jonson in nineteenth-century literary criticism and theatre. Jonson's characters certainly lack the 'inwardness' of Shakespeare's. It is also true that Jonson's method involves a degree of caricature, the exaggeration of one trait to the exclusion of others, and a tendency to see character from the outside. And, in *The Alchemist*, when the dust has finally settled, little seems to have changed, and the effect of Lovewit's adjudications at the end is really to fix the characters more or less where they started from: the world still runs on the same values of materialism and acquisitiveness, and Subtle and Doll have escaped over the garden wall to carry on their nefarious practices elsewhere. Jonson's conventions of characterization are clearly different from Shakespeare's, but it would be a mistake to assume that one was inherently more 'real' or 'convincing' than the other, since both are artificial.

The use of types as the basis for comic character is sanctioned by long dramatic tradition, as, almost from its ancient origins, comedy has dealt in typical characters representing the varieties of human folly. The influence of type characters from Roman comedy, for instance, can be seen in such characters as Face (the witty servant) or Kastril (an interesting variation on the *miles gloriosus* theme), and the tendency may also be coloured by allegorical characterization in the morality plays of native dramatic tradition. Contemporary literature also shows the popularity of character types in the manner of Theophrastus: Sir Thomas Overbury's *Characters* (1614) gives sketches of social types organized into bold outlines, and Jonson himself had felt able to preface one of his earlier plays with similar descriptions of his *dramatis personae*.

The Prologue (ll.7–11) to *The Alchemist* identifies the 'humours' of contemporary comedy with the traditional comic types. Asper, in the Induction to *Every Man out of his Humour*, gives voice to Jonson's objection to the popular use of the term 'humour' to describe the affectation of fantastical manners. It properly belongs to the medical theory that psychological states were physiologically induced. The predominance over the others of one of the four basic fluids or 'humours' present in the body – choler, blood, phlegm and bile – governed not only physical 'complexion' but also temperamental disposition to be choleric, sanguine, phlegmatic or melancholic. Jonson recognized that this could only be a metaphor for the dramatist's handling of comic character, so that in the theatrical context 'humour' means, in Asper's phrase, 'some one peculiar quality', some ruling obsession or passion, that comes to dominate a character. 'Sporting' with humours is an abiding concern of Jonson's comedies.

Finally, there are the names Jonson gives to his characters, which might seem to be little more than labels indicating type. Some denote social and economic function (Drugger); others, appearance and manner (Dapper, Surly). Yet others are more complex: Kastril (kestrel) is a sort of descriptive simile for the character's aggressiveness, with appropriate rural connotations; Ananias and Tribulation have names reflecting their religious persuasion, though with descriptive associations (Ananias 'cozened the Apostles', and tribulation will be their lot at the hands of Subtle and Face). Sir Epicure Mammon has the most complex name of all, pointing to his pride, self-indugence and worship of money. The very fact that he has two names, as well as a title, indicates something of the scale of his folly in a way that 'Abel Drugger' (tobacconist as ingenuous victim) and 'Tribulation Wholesome' (Anabaptists in moral crisis) do not.

We need to ask *how* Jonson uses the convention of type characters. Is the notion of 'humours' merely a convenient tool for the simplification, reduction or exaggeration of character? Coleridge felt that Jonson's characters were abstractions, distinguished from one another only 'by varieties and contrasts of manners'.[2] This view reflects a widespread feeling that it is the play's language, topical allusion, and detailed reference to urban and domestic life that sustain its vivid realism, while character remains schematic. The underlying assumption is of a playwright either less interested in individual human beings than in society, culture and language, or in the grip of the pessimism glimpsed in these words from *Discoveries*: 'Natures that are hardened to evil, you shall sooner break than make straight; they are like poles that are crooked and dry: there is no attempting them.' Such premises produce a reading of the play in which there is felt to be no organic life, and movement is a matter of plot mechanics, *imposing* change upon the characters.

But another kind of criticism has followed T. S. Eliot in questioning whether Jonson's characters are as lifeless as the crude theory of humours might suggest, since their total effect has a life at least as intense as that of Shakespeare's characters, even though it might be realized in different ways.[3] The vivid substance that permeates the play – the sense of the great city in its teeming life, and beyond it the towns and counties of England, the countryside of Kastril's estates and Lovewit's hopyards – acts not simply as a background or addition to characters, but as the very material from which they are formed, investing them with a convincing fullness. Face's description of Dapper (I.ii.50–8), for example, imbues the lawyer's clerk with a life beyond Theophrastian convention, and the effect is amplified by Dapper himself:

> I had a scurvy writ or two to make,
> And I had lent my watch last night to one

That dines today at the sheriff's, and so was robbed
Of my pass-time.

(I.ii.5–8)

The character gains not only the solidity of accurate social
'placing' but also an individual life from this feeble boasting
about the shabby glamour of his friendship with one
sufficiently distinguished to dine with the sheriff, and the
ownership of the watch (which may or may not exist). The
technique, reminiscent of a great novelist such as Dickens, is
seen everywhere in the play. Drugger brings on to the stage
with him the same kind of solidity, with his worms, hypo-
chondria and poor head for drink, all of which seem apt
accompaniments for his superstition, narrow ambition and
ingenuousness. In the same way, the economy of Drugger's
account of Kastril (II.vi.57–62) should not be thought of as
refining the would-be gallant into an anonymous type: when
we see him, we understand the full poignancy of what has been
described – the fantastical affectation of the 'roaring boy'
rooted in a provincial anxiety to be thought fashionable. Even
the most minor character can be given the spark of life by the
deft use of social or domestic detail, as when the sixth neighbour says

I heard a doleful cry,
As I sat up a-mending my wife's stockings.

(V.i.33–4)

What, then, is the role of 'humours' in the play? Jonson's
method of characterization examines the relationship between
men seen in their reality and complexity as social beings and
the ruling mannerisms, obsessions and passions that can come
to dominate them; between what makes them fully human and
what reduces them to humour or type. This peculiarly
Jonsonian analysis of character is illustrated in the following
exchange:

Sub. 'Pray God your sister prove but pliant.

Kas.   Why,
     Her name is so. . . . Knew you not that?
Sub.   No, faith, sir.
     Yet by erection of her figure I guessed it.
                                              (IV.iv.89–92)

The joke stems from the collision of the human being and the
name/label. We are made to contemplate the possibility, at
once comic and frightening, that the cony-catchers may be
right in their confident assumption that people are knowable,
predictable, mere types and humours.

Characterization is therefore a process, and one that provides
the very subject matter of the play. The dupes enter Lovewit's
house, and the play, with recognizable identities formed, as we
have seen, in a convincingly 'real' social world. Subtle and Face
then alchemize them, as it were, into their quintessence as
fools, greedy and gullible. Characterization, like alchemy itself,
is a process that moves the complex impurity of human life
towards its pure state: the humour, the type of human folly.
We are reminded that the theory of the four humours determining the complexion of human bodies was closely related to
the theory, fundamental to alchemy, of the four elements
determining the nature of material substances. The art of Subtle
and Face is that of character development, as they penetrate to
the vanity or greed in the heart of each of the dupes, encourage
its growth into fantasy, and fix it as a simple, predictable
humour, untrammelled by anything that might hamper the
exploitation of the victim.

Drugger's modest commercial scheme expands to include the
projected marriage, disguised as a Spanish count, into the
landed family of Kastril; Dapper's dreams of success at the
tables become enlarged into a self-delusion so complete that he
can be sold the fantasy of the Fairy Queen's favour; the
Anabaptists come to the point of predicting supreme secular
power for themselves. The voracious greed of Mammon, the
most energetic self-deluder of all, needs no encouragement
from the rogues: it is almost as if it is Mammon's imagination

and will that have created the whole alchemical pantomime, and not the wit of Subtle. He is a fool on a grand scale, and they decorously devise for him a fantasy involving social rank, unlimited wealth and power, and unrestrained lasciviousness. It takes the form of a sentimental tragedy, complete with mad noblewoman, her lordly brother hot to avenge the outraged honour of his house, and the apparent death through moral disappointment of a saintly philosopher. The external action of the play therefore comes to be possessed by the dupes' inner lives. Like the dupes themselves, the play is rooted in the grubby realities of London life, but impelled into the shape of their fantasies, acted out with the masterly help of three confidence tricksters in their various roles and disguises. Characterization is thus integral to the mock-heroic scheme of the play: various allusions to the 'high' kinds of literature, heroic romance (especially *The Faerie Queene*, echoes of which are eventually bodied forth in Doll's grotesque impersonation of the Fairy Queen herself) and tragedy (*The Spanish Tragedy* intrudes as both quotation and Hieronimo's costume), suggest aspirations to nobility in absurd contrast to the 'low' decorum of comedy.

That the alchemizing of character into humour is also a release into the realm of pure comedy reminds us once again of the art of the comic dramatist behind the art of Subtle. Henri Bergson, in his celebrated essay on *Laughter*,[4] defines the essence of comedy as 'mechanical inelasticity' of character, a failure to adapt to the constantly changing demands of life, especially social life. Such 'rigidity' gives to the actions and speech of the character a quality of automatism, and our laughter is provoked by the perception that human beings have become like machines. Jonson's characters may be seen as purely comic in this way, since, lacking self-knowledge, they relentlessly pursue their absurd delusions and fixed ideas. Thus Ananias is almost unstoppable in his dogmatic objections to popery and worldliness in III.ii, and Subtle is able to use him as a comic automaton to help drive Surly off the stage (IV.vii.42 ff.). It is one of the supremely funny moments of the play ('Thou look'st like Antichrist in that lewd hat'). Indeed, all of the dupes allow themselves in some way or another to become marionettes in the hands of their deceivers. This is particularly noticeable in the case of the inarticulate Drugger, who is moved around the stage and supplied with suitable responses by Face ('That's a secret, Nab!'), and of the increasingly bemused Dapper (see III.v).

Bergson also argues that comic characters are necessarily types or generalizations; partly because they are seen from the standpoint of social acceptability, and partly because the type is a reduction of the fully human, the mechanical usurping the living being. But Bergson also insists that some dimension of convincing life must cling to the comic character in order to serve as a foil for the 'inelastic' element, since it is the contrast between the living and the automatic that is laughable. This well describes Jonson's method in *The Alchemist*.

The controlling irony of all these characterizations is that, although the dupes come to Subtle to have the meanness of inadequate lives transmuted into the glamour of success and wealth, the only change they undergo in reality is to become more like themselves, to have their essential nature distilled into a simple humour. The process is both a moral analysis, in that it exposes their greed and selfishness, and a comic sporting with folly. In it, the two powerful impulses of Jonson's imagination – to a detailed realism on the one hand and incisive moral judgement on the other – are fused into a comic vision.

Yet there is a darker side to the play's treatment of the theme of identity which becomes apparent in the opening scene as a disturbing sense of the vulnerability of human personality. Here Face and Subtle each claim to have created the other out of an anonymous, bestial foulness. Thus Subtle

> went pinned up in the several rags
> You'd raked and picked from dunghills before day,
> Your feet in mouldy slippers for your kibes,
> A felt of rug, and a thin threaden cloak
> That scarce would cover your no-buttocks –

> (I.i.33–7)

and Face is repaid in kind by Subtle. Both claim to have provided the other with the wherewithal of identity, face and name: 'I ga' you count'nance,' Face tells Subtle; 'Slave, thou hadst had no name' is his rejoinder. A suggestion of blasphemy attaches to the idea of creation here, as each assumes the posture of a god facing his disobedient and ungrateful creature. 'Do you rebel?' asks Subtle; 'He ever murmurs,' complains Face – words that are resonant of the Old Testament accounts of Adam and Israel in their disobedience.

For Subtle, the creation of Face's identity is most readily described in alchemical terms (I.i.68–71), but their quarrel, as Doll reminds them, threatens to transmute them into the types of folly, like their dupes (I.i.163–6). Their quarrel mended, at least for the time being, they are free to fly up as volatile spirits, assuming the dazzling series of identities that controls the action of the play. If we ask what it is that places them in such command of their own and others' identities, the answer must partly lie in the self-knowledge that they force upon one another in this first scene. This, as Doll points out to them, is the difference between the cozener and the cozened (I.i.122–4).

Face's accomplished shape-shifting is reflected in the wide range of manners he adopts with his gulls, from servility with Mammon to insouciant condescension with Dapper. He exercises all the nimble trickery of the Ulenspiegel of German folk legend, whose name he adopts. He is always ready to 'shift', a word that means both 'to resort to some strategem' and 'to change clothes'. Indeed, the most obvious sign of Face's manipulation of his own identity is his use of disguise, alternating between the sooty rags of Lungs the laboratory drudge and the uniform of Captain Face, the worldly-wise denizen of tavern, street and ordinary. The stage convention, honoured in innumerable Renaissance plays, that disguise is impenetrable, emphasizes the completeness with which Face assumes and discards identities. He takes this convention to its limits –

> O, for a suit
> To fall now like a curtain, flap!
>
> (IV.ii.6–7)

– but it cannot contain him: even though he has been shaven to become 'smooth Jeremy', and nobody else seems able to connect him with Face, Dapper is induced to mistake him for 'the Captain' at V.iv.7. Such moments in the play remind the audience of the theatre itself as a place of shape-shifting, *deceptio visus* and, perhaps, cozenage. Lovewit's 'Peace, and get hence, you changelings' (V.ii.44) emphasizes that even his neighbours have no consistency, and may wittily cue the exit for a quick costume change of three actors doubling as Kastril, Ananias and Tribulation.

Subtle too plays a large number of parts, though they are more readily unified under his master art of alchemy: reverend doctor and astrologer, palmist, expert on duelling and marriage broker, and (it is hinted) abortionist and dispenser of quack remedies for venereal diseases. Doll also shares in this protean quality: the 'Doll Common' who can be in the eyes of her confederates 'Royal Doll' easily accomplishes the transformations into mad gentlewoman and Fairy Queen. Their shape-shifting begets vastly entertaining performances in their numerous adopted roles, but its very success seems to call into question the permanence of human personality in a deeply unsettling way.

Critics of the play have disagreed over whether the characters excite the audience's sympathy or contempt. Does the detailed realism of their presentation disgust us by its sordidness, or move us to compassion? Do their humours of self-delusion and greed deserve moral opprobrium or tolerant excuse? Behind such questions loom prejudices about Jonson himself, as becomes apparent in a discussion of Jonson's characters by the eighteenth-century critic Corbyn Morris.[5] Morris makes it perfectly clear where he stands, stating his preference for the 'joy, frolic and happiness' of Shakespeare's comedies over what he feels is the heavy didacticism of Jonson's. Thus

> Jonson, by pursuing the most useful intention of comedy, is in justice obliged to hunt down and demolish his own characters. Upon this plan he must necessarily expose

them to your hatred, and of course can never bring out an amiable person. His Subtle and Face are detested at last, and become mean and despicable. Sir Epicure Mammon is properly tricked, and goes off ridiculous and detestable. The puritan elders suffer for their lust of money, and are quite nauseous and abominable.

Equally, to emphasize the glamorous and amoral energy of Face, Subtle and Doll, and the pathos or splendour of their victims, might indicate the covert substitution for Morris's anti-Shakespearian pedant of a Jonson rehabilitated to reflect more modern prejudices; morally relaxed, or subversive rather than judgemental. But unbiased study of the play yields a more complex effect, as Corbyn Morris himself was forced to admit when he considered whether the prospect of Drugger, 'wrung between greediness to get money, and reluctance to part with money for that purpose', was 'mean and despicable', or whether

> his eager desire of getting and saving money, by methods he thinks lawful, are excusable in a person of his business; he is therefore not odious or detestable, but harmless and inoffensive in private life; and from thence ... he is the most capable of any of Jonson's characters of being a favourite in the theatre.

And theatrical favourite he was, even in the rather overstated performances of Theophilus Cibber that Morris had seen. Several great actors have excelled in the role, including Armin (who created the part), Garrick and Guinness.

In his indecision, Morris comes nearest to the truth. Our response to these characters is bound to be complex. If their mean lives beget a measure of compassion in varying degrees, the elements of physical grossness may also disgust. Their greed and folly are contemptible, but we may also sympathize with their plight as victims, both of others and of themselves. George Meredith (in *An Essay on Comedy*, 1897), Bergson, and other theorists of the comic, maintain that excess of any emotion, especially sympathy but also hatred or disgust, is inimical to the distancing necessary to comedy. Comedy depends upon a rational and broadly social point of view: too much compassion, too much contempt, and the comic spirit is dead. The contradictory impulses of Jonson's imagination are best seen as balancing and restraining one another to preserve the comic equation. Drugger, for example, possesses the pathos of the clown, which is entirely consonant with comedy. 'Did you never see me play the fool?' he asks, drawing attention to the great comic actor Robert Armin behind the character.

Above all, the sharpness, perceived by some critics as savagery, of Jonson's satire, is balanced by the sheer theatrical presence and comic vitality of his characters. This is obviously true of the rogues, but equally so of a character such as Mammon. He is a monster of selfishness, but also immensely attractive. There is an element of the mock-heroic in such characters that carries with it a double effect. The grand titles affected by the rogues ('Sovereign', 'General', 'Royal Doll') turn a satiric irony against them because they are so grotesquely inappropriate, but in a curious way these also match the triumphs of wit they accomplish. There is a mock-heroic grandeur about Mammon, too, that directs the irony against his greed and sensuality, but at the same time conveys a sense of exhilaration in Jonson's inflation of the repulsive to the point of magnificence.

LANGUAGE

Language is a distinctive feature of the play, and an important issue within it. Jonson uses the play's language for the satiric purpose of creating the standards against which the audience will measure the action and characters. There are, for example, significant patterns of imagery that establish the basis of moral judgement. Doll's conceit of the 'venture tripartite' being a common weal or 'republic' threatened by the 'faction' (civil disorder) of the quarrel in the opening scene is part of a whole system of political reference running through the play. Allusions to public officials (constables, marshals, sheriffs, magistrates, kings), national and local government, liveried companies, the Church, public philanthropy and private charity, serve to remind us of what society ideally should be like, and to create an irony through which we may contemplate its present tendency to collapse and disintegration as represented in the antisocial activities of the various characters. Similarly, the religious resonances of alchemical language are linked to numerous religious allusions throughout the play. Mammon, whose very surname indicates a false religion of money ('Ye cannot serve God and Mammon'; Matthew 6:24), persistently blasphemes in biblical allusions that associate him with attributes and powers of the Godhead, such as creation, resurrection, immortality and miraculous healing. An example of this religious resonance being realized as a specific dramatic situation comes in the following dialogue, which exposes a confusion of worldly and religious values that is at once richly comic and satirically pointed:

> Sur. Why, I have heard he must be *homo frugi*,
>   A pious, holy and religious man,
>   One free from mortal sin, a very virgin.
> Man. That makes it, sir, he is so. But I buy it.
>   (II.ii.97–100)

The effect is extended in II.iii, where Subtle and Mammon address each other as Catholic confessor and acolyte ('Father', 'son'), treating Surly as a 'heretic'. The comic effect of Subtle's solemn speech (II.iii.4–23), warning against covetousness and 'carnal appetite' as threats to 'so great and catholic a bliss' as alchemical success, ironically emphasizes the failure in the play's world of all the values he mentions: patience, love, zeal, altruism, piety and charity.

Equally if not more important is the way in which language is made to *enact* the spiritual vulgarity, moral confusion and social disintegration of the play's world. Jonson writes extensively in *Discoveries* (and elsewhere) on language, and it holds a central place in his vision of man and society: 'Speech is the only benefit man hath to express his excellency of mind above other creatures. It is the instrument of society.' Furthermore, the condition of language will reflect the state of a man's mind, and of society as a whole: 'Wheresoever manners and fashions are corrupted, language is. It imitates the public riot. The excess of feasts and apparel are the notes of a sick state; and the wantonness of language, of a sick mind.' Since the essential condition of the play's world is its incoherence, it is not surprising to find language itself reflecting the tendency to social fragmentation in a range of competing jargons, and to individual isolation in solipsism and fantasy.

Each character or (in the case of the Anabaptists, the neighbours and the elves) group has its own distinctive speech and vocabulary: Dapper's law terms; Drugger's vocabulary of trade and city; Kastril's rustic dialect, colouring the metropolitan roaring boys' argot that he affects; the underworld cant of the confidence tricksters; and the Anabaptists' religious cant. Jonson attached great importance to decorum, the matching of character and speech in the drama. 'Words', he says in *Discoveries*, 'are to be chose according to the persons we make speak, or the things we speak of.' In *The Alchemist* he observes the fascinating but perverse decorum of a world that is falling apart. The Anabaptists provide a clear example of this, being, literally, separatists who reject state authority and the established church, and pose a political threat to traditional social order. Their outlandish, canting speech, based largely on the language of the Old Testament, and relying heavily on such words as 'spirit' and 'zeal', isolates the 'exiled saints' in an aggressive sub-group seeking to dignify itself with a spurious piety. It is hypocritical and delusive, in that it cloaks the sacrifice of their pretended principles to fantasies of secular power.

Above these socially derived jargons is another level of more exotic and specialized languages adopted as disguises, so to speak, in the furtherance of the various deceptions. Although intelligible to those who use them, they tend to be incomprehensible to others. Such, for example, are the vocabularies of Subtle's arcane specialisms, conjuring, necromancy, chiromancy, astrology, and so forth, all subsumed under the master jargon of alchemy, the main point of which, as he explains to Surly, is to *conceal* meaning (II.iii.198–210). The tendency to limit the communicative power of language is also seen in Surly's Spanish, which Face and Subtle do not understand, in Doll's genealogical ravings, and, in its extreme form, in the twittering of the imaginary elves conjured to torment Dapper. Exaggeration and parody play their part in the formation of these languages, of course, but where we can check them against his sources (Delrio on alchemy, Broughton on biblical genealogy, various handbooks on duelling) we find that Jonson is surprisingly faithful to the 'language such as men do use'.

Readers who sometimes complain that understanding and enjoyment of the play are hampered by an excessive linguistic obscurity miss the point of Jonson's dramatic use of language. His verbal art here aspires to the condition of a mad, abstract music which signifies the death of meaning at the hands of folly. This central theme takes on an ominous dimension through allusions to the Bible. Mammon's 'Be rich', the 'word' that will create men anew and transform the world into a golden paradise, parodies the divine fiat by which the world is created in chapter 1 of Genesis, and the all-creating Word that is Christ at the beginning of John's gospel. Particularly relevant is the account of Pentecost (Acts 2), when the spirit of God, like a 'rushing mighty wind' and in tongues of fire, comes upon the Apostles, causing them to address, and be understood by, a multilingual crowd: such is the transformational power of God's word, that three thousand are immediately converted. The linguistic cacophony of the play, however, inverts Pentecost into its anti-type, Babel (Genesis 11). The attempt to build the tower of Babel up to heaven symbolizes an overweening human aspiration, and God's punishment was to confound the one language in the world into a confusion of tongues.

Mammon gives supreme expression to the solipsism and

fantasy that infect all the gulls in some measure. Not for nothing will his court poets be those 'that writ so subtly of the fart', for his own rhetoric is, quite literally, inflated:

> I will have all my beds blown up, not stuffed:
> Down is too hard.
>
> (II.ii.41–2)

The speech continues through mists, perfume, vapour, flattery, fans and wind, to reach its climax with 'the swelling unctuous paps / Of a fat pregnant sow'; and he is attended by Face, addressed as 'Puff' and 'Lungs', the alchemist's bellows-man, reminding us of the wind and fire of the play's ironic Pentecost. *The Alchemist* itself begins with Subtle's fart, and the alchemical swindle ends with the great gusts of Doll's talking fit, followed by the explosion of the furnace and 'All the works / ... flown *in fumo*'.[6] Interestingly enough, Mammon brings this catastrophe upon himself as much by his linguistic habits as his greed and lechery, for it is his inability, despite Face's warning, to resist yet another of his blasphemous biblical allusions (this time to a 'fifth monarchy') in his fulsome wooing of Doll that triggers her unstoppable outburst.

In these ways, language acts as the instrument of Jonson's satiric purpose. The experience of reading the play, however, and certainly that of seeing it well acted, will surely convince us that Jonson regards the jargons of the play with as much fascination as horror. Recent criticism of the play has suggested that the self-contained world for which a jargon speaks resembles in some respects the imaginary world created by the poet, and that the solipsistic verbal fantasies of Mammon reflect at least a distorted image of the proud and aloof genius of Jonson himself.[7] No matter that we are talking here of parody, mock-heroic and hyperbole; the creative energy of Mammon, Doll and Face's speeches, and the distinctiveness of (for instance) Kastril's, communicate Jonson's exhilaration as much as they stimulate ours.

Becoming intoxicated by language is not confined to Mammon, but extends to Face –

> thou shalt keep him waking with thy drum –
> Thy drum, my Doll, thy drum! – till he be tame
>
> (III.iii.44–5)

– and to Subtle:

> in your *bathada*
> You shall be soaked, and stroked, and tubbed, and rubbed,
> And scrubbed, and fubbed, dear Don, before you go.
> You shall, in faith, my scurvy baboon Don,
> Be curried, clawed, and flawed, and tawed, indeed.
>
> (IV.iii.96–100)

His characters here are surely sharing in Jonson's own delight in words. 'What a brave language here is, next to canting!' (II.iii.42).

The play also equates the workings of language with the process of alchemy. The fragmentary biblical history of language contained in Doll's ravings, the theory that language developed from a 'primitive tongue' spoken by Adam (Mammon thinks it was High Dutch, Ananias favours Hebrew), strongly resembles Subtle's exposition of the alchemical theory that physical substances evolved from 'remote matter'. Language is the true philosopher's stone in the play, transmuting the raw material of experience into the refined substance of poetry; and there is a pervasive sense that a linguistic substratum of randomly accumulated nouns is being developed into the dazzling syntax of the great set speeches of Subtle and Mammon. The audience, as well as the gulls, are made to appreciate how short-lived are the glorious illusions alchemized by words: where the audience had been led to imagine a laboratory behind the scenes, they are told at last of

> A few cracked pots and glasses, and a furnace;
> The ceiling filled with poesies of the candle,
> And madam with a dildo writ o' the walls.
>
> (V.v.40–2)

To complain of a linguistic swindle does not fully meet the case, as Surly discovers. His rejoinder to Subtle's great *tour de force* of alchemical apologetics (II.iii.142–76) is, in its way, vigorous and witty, listing forty-four alchemical terms and substances in one sentence that itself threatens to 'burst a man' to speak (II.iii.182–98). As a statement of the incomprehensibility of Subtle's mumbo-jumbo, and a vision of the chaos of unrelated things that is the reality behind the alchemical illusion, it has an almost prophetic effectiveness. But Subtle wins the contest easily, and Surly has to re-enter the drama on Subtle's terms, disguised and speaking an incomprehensible language. While obviously thinking more quickly than Surly, Subtle can also produce an energetic syntax, where Surly offers only the stifling deadness of a list of words.

We are bound to respond more readily to those characters who display in their use of words the element of comic *performance* that makes for stage presence. Indeed, there is a sense in which the obsessive talking of the play, reproached by the taciturn Surly, is one of the essential constituents of comedy. Some of the characters become what Bergson called 'talking machines', churning out words with machine-like prolixity. 'Whom the disease of talking still once possesseth, he can never hold his peace ... too much talking is ever the indice of a fool', Jonson notes in *Discoveries*, an observation that well describes the verbal juggernaut that Mammon has become as a result of his undeviating pursuit of his delusions. Some of the most striking 'talking machines' of the play are actually devised by the rogues as instruments with which to triumph over their victims. Something of this is seen in the alchemical catechism performed 'i' the language' by Face and Subtle to impress and intimidate Ananias (II.v.18–45); but the most perfect example is Doll's inexorable talking fit (IV.v.1–32). The fact that the mechanical talking is consciously assumed rather than unconsciously compelled does not seem to affect the Bergsonian sense of the comic: we laugh because we are made to perceive the human being as a machine. Surly actually becomes trapped inside a Spanish talking machine of his own devising.

DENOUEMENT

The desire for 'poetical justice', as Dr Johnson acknowledged when contemplating the ending of *King Lear*, is a very powerful impulse in the human mind. 'A play in which the wicked prosper, and the virtuous miscarry' may well be 'a just representation of the common events of human life', but it offends the natural love of justice in 'all reasonable beings'.[8] Criticism of *The Alchemist* gives ample evidence of this in its persistent search for some kind of acceptable moral fable within the play, an enterprise for which the play's ending is bound to prove a stumbling-block. Dryden questioned whether comic dramatists had ever observed any law requiring comedy 'to reward virtue and punish vice', and cited the ending of *The Alchemist* as an example:

> where Face, after having contrived and carried on the great cozenage of the play, and continued it without repentance to the last, is not only forgiven by his master, but enriched by his consent with the spoils of those whom he has cheated. And, which is more, his master himself, a grave man and a widower, is introduced taking this man's counsel, debauching the widow first in hope to marry her afterward. (Preface to *An Evening's Love*, 1671)

And, if we are not deterred from the quest for a punitive or at least judgemental denouement by Dryden, the play itself contains its own warnings in the form of parodies of moralized endings. The first of these occurs in IV.v, where the explosion of the furnace seems like the anger of heaven –

> as if a bolt
> Of thunder had been driven through the house!
> (IV.v.59–60)

– and Mammon cries out, 'O my voluptuous mind! I am justly punished' (IV.v.74). But it is all another illusion created in furtherance of the confidence trick. In a somewhat different way, Surly intends his emergence from the Spanish disguise in

IV.vi to be the triumph of plain truth and the end of cozenage; and, though Face and Subtle 'reel' momentarily, Face is able to turn the tables on him by persuading Kastril, aided by Drugger and Ananias, to quarrel him off the stage (IV.vii.1–58). Face's 'Nothing's more wretched than a guilty conscience' (V.ii.47) and 'Hark you, thunder' (V.iv.137) might be thought to inject the same note of parody into the real denouement.

The best hope for 'poetical justice' in the resolution of the plot would seem to lie with 'normative characters' who sustain or impose positive standards. Surly and Lovewit, both plain-speaking men ('The truth, the shortest way,' demands Lovewit) are the obvious candidates. But Surly is hardly an exemplary character, being a professional cardsharp, commodity swindler and pimp (II.i.9–14). He is slow-witted, coarse of speech, crude and unsympathetic in his judgements, and his motives are impure and confused. His 'foolish vice of honesty' expresses no principle higher than a gambler's determination not to be cheated, and his campaign to expose deception becomes confused with his self-interested involvement with the Widow Pliant. His failure is foreshadowed in the unconscious irony of his boast:

> Faith, I have a humour:
> I would not willingly be gulled. Your stone
> Cannot transmute me.
>
> (II.i.77–9)

His refusal to be alchemized into a humour is itself a humour.

Lovewit, on the other hand, is invested with the authority of master of the house and the character who presides over the denouement. Yet, as his name seems to indicate, he represents the final triumph of the amoral intelligence of the rogues, for it is his 'love [of] a teeming wit' that leads him to pardon Face and to continue, by more socially acceptable means, the nimble opportunism of the 'venture tripartite'. His name might, of course, be decoded as an alliance of wit and love, intelligence and charity, and so stand for an enlightened social morality. The leniency of his treatment of rogues and victims alike, though not perhaps very even-handed, certainly looks charitable in some loose sense, but it could not be called disinterested benevolence. Does he stand for a moral realism, accommodating virtuous ends (marriage, the restoration of order) within practical methods? His little lecture (V.v.50–8) to the downcast Surly after he has filched the widow from him, ridiculing his attempts to behave honourably with Pliant, may be thought rather too close to other grubby compromisers of principle in the play, such as the Anabaptists, for him to be considered as the exemplar of enlightened self-interest.

Can the ending of the play be moralized without 'normative characters'? The plot could be seen as a sort of self-righting mechanism, in which the rogues expose the fools and then, overreaching themselves, are overthrown in their turn. Knavery and folly cancel each other out, and the natural balance of society reasserts itself. That balance, however, has not much about it of civilization's 'sweetness and light' and seems to allow a moral complacency to the audience that is difficult to reconcile with Jonson's demand for the exercise of judgement.

An alternative reading of the last act sees it as the triumph, not of moral or political principles, but of the 'comic spirit', making it a play of celebration rather than judgement. The ending of The Alchemist certainly lacks the spirit of reconciliation, social integration and restoration that, as the accompaniment of the emergence of a new social order based on youthful energy and marriage, is the sine qua non of comedy in Northrop Frye's influential theory.[9] Lovewit's marriage to Pliant and restoration of social order have only to be compared with the ending of (say) Twelfth Night or As You Like It to take the measure of The Alchemist's ironic divergence from that type of comedy. But the 'spirit of comedy' can also be credibly identified with the witty intrigue of Roman New Comedy, where the spirit is one of anarchy, directed against authority, social order and conventional morality. Indeed, a triumph such as that of the clever slave Tranio in Plautus' Mostellaria, and his ultimate forgiveness by his master, can be linked to carnival and Saturnalia, which temporarily disrupted established order, allowing slave, servant and others in lowly positions a brief festive reign over those normally in authority. The vindication of the unscrupulous Face by his equally unscrupulous master, which goes beyond forgiveness to active approval, certainly has the effect of overturning social and moral conventions. The censorious Jonson of 'To the Reader' might appear to have been vanquished by his unofficial self, celebrating imagination, wit and vitality, as repelled by the shrunken and joyless morality of Surly as he is by the hypocrisy of the Anabaptists.

The two constituents of the Horatian formula that Jonson applied to comedy, its capacity to *delight* and its duty to *teach*, seem to have drifted irreconcilably apart. Is it possible to reassemble *The Alchemist* as a didactic comedy in which laughter and judgement are interdependent? One possibility might lie in considering the positive function that carnival, Saturnalia and holiday have always had in reinforcing the orthodoxies which they are briefly allowed to subvert: the excess of disorder and licence usually illuminates the necessity for order and restraint. Apart from the ironic suggestions of the verse, Jonson's image of the times provides us with no absolutely trustworthy characters, and no really convincing operative justice in the plot. The Judging Spectators have to look outside the play, and especially to themselves, for positive standards. We see in the play's satiric mirror a world of rogues and fools designed to provoke just such a response.

A version of what this response might entail is hinted at by the way in which Jonson leads his readers into the printed text of the play. Readers start with the dedicatory epistle to Lady Wroth, invoked as the apotheosis of an ideal aristocratic virtue, as absolutely herself in virtue as the dupes of the play are in folly. They then find an idealized image of themselves in 'To the Reader', engaged in the heroic labour of understanding, a scholarly quest for truth undertaken far from the cozenage of the theatre. Then, after a list of dramatis personae and an acrostic summary of the plot, they encounter the Prologue's theory of comedy, claiming theatrical experience for moral edification. Finally, they come to the play's explosive opening line, at the opposite extreme from the odoriferous incense that the poet had burnt before Lady Wroth. Readers, in other words, descend to the play through a Platonic hierarchy; and, although the play's inverted world demolishes it, Jonson suggests that their response, if it is the right one, can re-erect the social and moral pyramid. If they have their wits about them, the play's *speculum vitae* might lead them into serious thought about themselves and society. Jonson argues in *Discoveries* that comedy functions in this way provided that 'the manners of the reader be once in safety'.

In opening the question whether the spectators should 'own' (that is, acknowledge) the follies of the play as theirs, the Prologue assumes that they will become part of a hierarchy of self-knowledge that begins within the play and extends beyond it. The dupes are completely unselfconscious, easily deluded by foolish desire. Above them is Surly, knowing enough to recognize cozenage when he sees it, but not in command of his own impurity of motive. The success of the rogues in manipulating others surely stems from the thorough knowledge they have of themselves, painfully rehearsed in the first scene. They are dishonest, but at least they do not share the hypocrisy of the Anabaptists. At the top of the play's hierarchy is Lovewit, fully aware of himself and where his advantage lies: prudent, tolerant, unscrupulous. The spectators' ability to see the limitations of a character such as Lovewit will depend upon the degree of self-knowledge they have, or the kind of self-examination that the play will provoke. The effect of the play will be not so much to *bring out* our folly as to make us aware of our potential for it and resolve to amend.

> If I see anything that toucheth me, shall I come forth a betrayer of myself presently? No; if I be wise, I'll dissemble it; if honest, I'll avoid it: lest I publish that on my own forehead, which I saw there noted without a title.
> (*Discoveries*)

Jonson aims not to alchemize his spectators into the foolish humours of the play but to 'heighten' them (as the alchemists would say) into virtue. Where the dupes had been turned inside out to expose their foolish inner parts to our laughter, the play seeks to turn the spectator inward, and make self-knowledge the foundation of wisdom.

However, the ideal workings of Sidney's theory of comedy, although available to the reader who has been warned of the theatre as a place of cozenage, might not so readily accord to the audience's experience of the play in the theatre. The performed play might not be as easy to control for didactic purposes as the text in the cool perspective of the study. Jonson, great dramatist that he is, knows that the democracy of the playhouse – the intervention of the actor's interpretation and the volatility of the audience – moves plays away from the intentions of even the most autocratic author. He acknowledges this by investing his characters with the extraordinary *theatricality* that makes them at once so enjoyable and threateningly ambiguous. The final speeches of Lovewit and Face, as they step outside the dramatic illusion and speak directly to the audience, bring the unmoralized aspects of the theatrical experience into clear focus. Lovewit asks us to excuse his straining of candour and violations of comic decorum as the price of his newly acquired wife. Face, on the other hand, blames comic decorum for mitigating his triumph in the last act, and asks for our applause in approval of his accomplishments. The mockery of the language of neo-classical literary criticism ('decorum') is matched by a similarly ironic use of the language of forensic judgement (Face appeals to us, a jury of his countrymen, to acquit him). Face's teasing manner is reminiscent of that of Folly in Erasmus's *Praise of Folly* (1509), or of the Vice of the morality plays: above all, it calls to mind the solicitations of applause at the end of Plautus' comedies. To applaud is to admit complicity with rogues, or perhaps a confession of folly; to admit that you have loved wit more than justice; to admit that the laws of comic form, and morality itself, might not be as relevant as we at first thought.

Face's invitation to 'new guests' creates another disturbing inference about the connection between aesthetic and moral judgement. If, as the preface 'To the Reader' suggests, the corrupt standards of playwrights and audiences have made the popular theatre a swindle that defrauds people of judgement, what guarantee have we that *The Alchemist* has not duped us? The play was probably performed at the Blackfriars 'private house' (as well as at the Globe), and Jonson wittily sets the play at a house in the Blackfriars and makes its action contemporaneous with its first production in 1610. The audience, like Subtle's dupes, have been persuaded to part with their money in exchange for mere illusions conjured by Jonson's alchemical theatre. There is an alternative to being fooled into crude enjoyment and the laughter stirred by 'mean affections', but Surly's glum philistinism provides an unattractive image of the ignorant and pretentious critic that Jonson so despised: the sceptical wiseacre in the audience, disinclined to believe any of it. And Lovewit, whose social peers must have been numerous in the Blackfriars audience, presents a picture of clever self-possession that is, on reflection, hardly flattering.

But the final effect of Face's ironies may not be to sweep away all pretence at civilized standards of judgement, but to open out the question of the aesthetic and moral basis of comedy. We gain a refreshing sense of Jonson's own hesitations, uncertainties and divisions as he allows us to contemplate the subversive possibilities surrounding his moral comedy: that ''Tis all *deceptio visus*'; that the triumph of the carnival spirit of comedy, of the underdog and the lawless impulse, may be sometimes so complete as to expose the absurdity of all human attempts at justice and order. Instead of offering us a homiletic drama, Jonson exploits a kind of raw, risky excitement in the vicarious experience of trickery as a device to educate his audience, and maybe himself, in humane understanding. Morality becomes, in the end, a matter not for books and plays but for people, and the task of judgement not impossible or reductive but exacting, demanding both honesty and humanity.

NOTES

1   S. T. Coleridge, *Table Talk* (1835); J. Dryden, *Of Dramatic Poesy* (1668). The relevant passages are reprinted in R. V.

Holdsworth, (ed.), *'Every Man in his Humour' and 'The Alchemist': A Casebook* (London, 1978), pp. 41–2, 148–9.

2 S. T. Coleridge, *Literary Remains* (1836); in Holdsworth (ed.), op. cit., pp. 51–2.

3 T. S. Eliot, 'Ben Jonson', *Selected Essays* (London, 1932).

4 Henri Bergson, *Laughter: An Essay on the Meaning of The Comic*, trans. C. Brereton and F. Rothwell (London, 1911).

5 Corbyn Morris, *An Essay towards Fixing the True Standards of Wit, Humour, Raillery, Satire, and Ridicule* (1744); in Holdsworth (ed.), op. cit., pp. 43–5.

6 For a discussion of the play's imagery of wind, fire, smoke, etc., and its relation to the theme of identity, see Ian Donaldson, 'Language, noise and nonsense', in Earl Miner (ed.), *Seventeenth Century Imagery* (Berkeley and London, 1971). See also the chapter on the play's imagery in E. B. Partridge, *The Broken Compass* (London, 1958).

7 See A. Leggatt, *Ben Jonson: His Vision and Art* (London and New York, 1981), pp. 18, 23 *et passim*.

8 *Johnson on Shakespeare*, ed. Arthur Sherbo (*The Yale Edition of the Works of Samuel Johnson*, vol. 8 (New Haven, 1968)), pp. 704–5.

9 As set out, for example, in Northrop Frye, *A Natural Perspective* (New York, 1965).

Select bibliography

EDITIONS

Herford, C. H., and Simpson, P. and E. (eds), *Ben Jonson*, 11 vols, Oxford, 1925–52. (This remains an invaluable resource for the study of Jonson. *The Alchemist* is in vol. V, with commentary and notes in vol. X. Vols I and II contain a biography and introductions to the plays.)

Mares, F. H. (ed.), *The Alchemist*, The Revels Plays, London and Cambridge, Mass., 1967. (A sound, scholarly edition with very full notes and excellent introduction.)

CRITICISM AND COMMENTARY

Bamborough, J. B., *Ben Jonson*, London, 1970. (An excellent introduction to the study of Jonson.)

Barton, A., *Ben Jonson, Dramatist*, Cambridge, 1984. (Contains an interesting account of *The Alchemist* as a play by Jonson the experimenter in comic form, increasingly drawn to the manner of Elizabethan comedy, despite his espousal of neo-classical principles.)

Donaldson, I., 'Ben Jonson', in *English Drama to 1710*, ed. C. Ricks, *Sphere History of Literature in the English Language*, vol. 3, London, 1971. (A short but stimulating introductory discussion of Jonson.)

Eliot, T. S., 'Ben Jonson', in *Selected Essays*, London, 1932. (Eliot's suggestions for a critical reappraisal altered the course of Jonson criticism.)

Gibbons, B., *Jacobean City Comedy*, 2nd edn, London and New York, 1980. (This influential book is good on the relation of this and other plays to their economic, social and political background, and gives an interesting exposition of *The Alchemist* as exemplar of this genre.)

Holdsworth R. V. (ed.), *'Every Man in his Humour' and 'The Alchemist': A Casebook*, London, 1978. (Includes a representative range of criticism from the late seventeenth century to 1971.)

Jackson, G. B., *Vision and Judgement in Ben Jonson's Drama*, New Haven, Conn., and London, 1968. (Discusses the working out through the plays' language and structure of Jonson's concepts of the poet and poetry.)

Leggatt, A., *Ben Jonson: His Vision and Art*, London and New York, 1981. (Attempting the 'intelligent saturation in [Jonson's] work as a whole' that Eliot thought essential, Leggatt's perceptive study is inevitably rather awkward to use in that it focuses not on individual works but on their interrelations.)

Partridge, E. B., *The Broken Compass: A Study of the Major Comedies of Ben Jonson*, London and New York, 1958. (Contains an analysis of the imagery and metaphorical language of *The Alchemist*.)

Riggs, D., *Ben Jonson: a Life*, Cambridge, Mass. and London, 1989. (This standard literary biography of Jonson gives a lucid, scholarly account of Jonson's life and works in historical context, with an interesting Freudian reading of his personality.)

Summers, C. J., and Pebworth, T., *Ben Jonson*, Twayne's English Authors Series, Boston, Mass., 1979. (A useful introductory survey of Jonson's life, times and writings.)

Thayer, C. G., *Ben Jonson: Studies in the Plays*, Norman, Oklahoma, 1963. (A clearly written study, concentrating on Jonson's commentary on his comic art, and the play's closer affinity with the Old Comedy than the New.)

Notes

TO THE LADY MOST DESERVING HER NAME, AND BLOOD:
MARY, LA[DY] WROTH

Title   *deserving* 'Wroth' was sometimes spelt, and probably
pronounced, 'Worth'.
Mary, La[dy] Wroth neice to Sir Philip Sidney and
daughter of the Earl of Leicester. She married Sir
Robert Wroth in 1604. Jonson wrote poetic encomia to
the Wroths and members of the Sidney family.

4   *gums* incense.

5   *hecatomb* a great public sacrifice.

7–8   *conscience* knowledge.

9–10   *your value ... remembers* the fact that you value it
which makes it a memorial of.

13   *assiduity* constant use.

16   *paint* use cosmetics.

TO THE READER

2–4   *takest up ... commodity* comparing contemporary
poetry and plays with the commodity swindle (see
II.i.10–14 n.).

3   *pretender* i.e. to knowledge.

5   *cozened* cheated, deceived.

6   *antics*   theatrical grotesquery.

7–8   *nature ... art*   In *Discoveries*, Jonson argues that nature
        is the end of art, and that bad art is divorced from
        nature.

9–10   *professors*   practitioners.

11   *naturals*   natural talents.

16   *excellent*   (used facetiously).
        judgement   censoriousness.

19   *braver*   (1) finer; (2) more courageous.

20   *rudeness*   uncouthness, lack of standards.

22   *foil*   defeat.

32   *suffrages*   votes.

34   *copy*   copiousness, substance.

35–6   *election ... mean*   judicious selection and moderation.

37   *scattered*   disorderly, random.

38   *numerous*   (1) abundant; (2) harmonious, metrically
        correct.
        composed   ordered, decorous.

THE PERSONS OF THE PLAY

15   *Mutes*   There is, in fact, only one non-speaking
        character, the Parson.

THE ARGUMENT

1   *The sickness hot*   the plague raging.

4   *punk*   prostitute.

10   *figures*   horoscopes.

11   *flies*   familiar spirits.

PROLOGUE

3   *Judging Spectators*   an ironic pun, (1) attacking hostile
        and ignorant criticism, and (2) appealing to informed
        judgement.

4   *ourselves* The King's Men, who first performed the play.

8   *squire* pimp.

9   *humours* essential bodily fluids. In the Introduction to *Every Man out of his Humour*, Jonson had objected to the use of this medical term to mean 'manners', defining *humour* as 'some one peculiar quality' that dominates character.

10   *still* always. Thus the play's London characters correspond to the 'type' characters of classical comedy.

11   *spleen* here in its more unusual sense of 'caprice'.

14   *above* beyond.

18   *correctives* medicines.

19   *apply* i.e. find allusions to living persons in the play.

24   *own* confess to.

ACT I, SCENE I

1   *Thy worst* Do your worst.

3   *figs* piles.

4   *out ... sleights* stop your tricks.

6   *gum ... silks* i.e. drench you. (Silk could be stiffened by the application of gum.)

7   *strong water* Subtle threatens Face with a vial of acid. *and* if.

10   *All ... made* The proverbial gibe at the parvenu or man of fashion is given added point by the fact that Face is a man of disguises.

16   *livery-three-pound-thrum* cheap, shabby servant.

17   *Friars* Blackfriars, part of the city of London. *The Alchemist* may have been acted at the Blackfriars theatre.

18   *vacations* between the legal terms, when the courts were not sitting.

19   *suburb-captain* Face's military rank is spurious.

22   *countenanced* (1) given credence; (2) favoured (with an implied play on Face's name).

23   *collect*   recollect.

25   *Pie Corner*   a locality of cooks' shops, near Smithfield.

28   *costive*   constipated.

         pinched-horn   like a shoehorn.

29   *Roman wash*   obscure: (1) swarthy, dirty (?); (2) a
         cosmetic (?).

31   *powder corns*   grains of gunpowder.

32   *advance ... voice*   speak louder (facetious).

35   *kibes*   chilblains.

36   *felt of rug*   coarse woollen hat.

51   *Make ... strange*   Do not pretend puzzlement.

51–3   As butler, Face should have distributed bread scraps
         (*chippings*) and dole beer to the poor through the
         buttery-hatch, but he has turned charity into profit.
         aqua-vitae men   sellers of spirits that they distilled from
         beer and wine.

54   *vails*   gratuities.

55   *post and pair*   a card game.

         counters   gambling chips.

56   *twenty marks*   £13. 6*s*. 8*d*., a mark being worth 13*s*. 4*d*.

59   *scarab*   dung beetle.

68–80   Subtle compares the raising of Face from butler to
         captain with the alchemical transformation of base
         metal into gold, and his rebellion with the explosion of
         a furnace at the very moment of perfection. For an
         explanation of the terms, see the Glossary.

85   *deaf John's*   presumably some low tavern.

90   *collier*   associated with cheating and the devil himself,
         and also appropriate to the alchemist's sooty visage.

91   *picture*   either (1) a graphic description or (2) a drawing.

93   *Paul's*   St Paul's Cathedral, where public notices were
         displayed.

94   *coz'ning ... scrapings*   i.e. secreting small quantities of
         silver or gold in a hollow coal in order to fake the
         process of transmutation of base metals.

95   *Searching ... shears*   a well-documented ritual used to
         find lost or stolen articles.

96	*Erecting ... houses* casting horoscopes.
	houses zodiac signs.
97	*taking ... glass* fortune-telling.
98	*red letters* i.e. giving added significance to the text of the notice.
	cut engraved.
99	*Gamaliel Ratsey* a highwayman who wore a hideous mask.
	sound sane.
101	*barely reckoning* merely listing.
102	*prove ... stone* i.e. enrich.
103	*trencher-rascal* scrounger.
	dog-leech dog-doctor.
106	*lying ... basket* i.e. being too greedy with prison food.
110	*republic* i.e. their joint venture.
111	*brach* bitch.
112–13	*statute... eight* the statute of 1541 prohibiting sorcery (including alchemy), which had been confirmed in 1604.
114	*laundering ... barbing* 'sweating' and clipping coins.
115	*coxcomb* the fool's headgear.
120	*marshal* the provost-marshal, in charge of the prison.
121	*dog-bolt* a blunt arrow (?) (obscure); used as an insult.
127	*apocryphal* inauthentic.
130	*give the cause* argue your case.
	insult exult.
131	*primacy ... divisions* major share of the spoils.
132–3	*you ... project with* you alone had the materials for alchemy.
137	*fall ... couples* hunt in pairs, like hounds.
139	*term* The legal terms were the busiest times in London (see I.i.18).
141	*part* share.
142	*objects his pains* complains about his labours.
160	*shark* cheat.
164	*precise* puritanical.

165   *king* James I had been seven years on the throne in 1610.

167   *ride* i.e. in a cart and be whipped, the whore's punishment.

168   *hole ... in* the pillory.

169   *pay ear-rent* have your ears cropped.

170   *Don Provost* the hangman, entitled to the clothes of his victims.

173   *crewel* worsted yarn, punning on 'cruel'.

174   *worsted* with a pun on 'cheated'.

175   *Claridiana* heroine of a popular Spanish romance, *The Mirror of Knighthood*.

177-9 *Common ... Particular* playing on grammatical terms, with sexual innuendo.
       cut straw (they will draw lots for her favours).

189   *quodling* unripe apple, hence 'green youth'.

191   *Dagger* a tavern.

192   *familiar* familiar spirit.

193   *rifle* gamble.

195   *as* as though.

ACT I, SCENE II

8   *pass-time* means of telling the time.

10   *broke with* confided in, mentioned (the matter) to.

11   *make the matter ... so dainty* consider the matter to be of such delicacy.

17   *Read* Simon Read was eventually pardoned in 1608 for having conjured spirits to locate stolen money.

26   *chiaus* from the Turkish *chaush*, 'messenger', synonymous with 'cheat' after Mustapha, a Turk, succeeded in having himself entertained as an ambassador of the Sultan at the expense of the Levant Company in London in 1607.

37-8   *angels ... spirits* gold coins worth about 10 shillings, with a conventional pun.

42   *a horse ... halter* i.e. to the gallows.

44   *difference of* distinction between.

46   *Clim o' the Cloughs* outlaw hero of ballads and romances.
        Claribels perhaps the amorous knight (Claribell) of Spenser's *Faerie Queene*, IV.ix.

47   *five-and-fifty and flush* an unbeatable hand in the card game primero.

50   *vicar* vicar-general, acting for a bishop in ecclesiastical courts.

51   *forty marks* £26. 13*s*. 4*d*.

55   *ciph'ring* accounting.

56   *Xenophon* Greek soldier and author; altered from *Testament* in the Quarto, perhaps to escape censorship. But Dapper may pass this secular book off as the Bible in order to avoid being bound by oaths.

58   *Ovid* Roman author (43 BC–AD 18) of *The Art of Love*.

61   *velvet head* (1) a doctor's velvet cap; (2) the antlers of a young stag, covered with 'velvet'.

63   *puck-fist* puff-ball (fungus).

69   *assumpsit* legal term for a verbal promise confirmed by the payment of money.

81   *play* gamble.
        set bet against.

97   *consideration* payment.

99–101 i.e. gamblers, having lost all to Dapper, will have to dine on credit at the eating-house (*ordinary*).

101   *conceive* understand.

109   *Holland ... Isaac* Isaac and John Hollandus, Dutch alchemists.

111–12 *put ... to a cloak* strip of all but their cloaks.

119   *happy* rich (Lat. *beatus*).

128   *caul* the foetal membrane; for it to be on the infant's head at birth was a sign of good fortune.

130   *I' fac* in faith.

135   *rate* behaviour.

151   *resolve* assure.

173   *twenty nobles* 6. 13*s*. 4*d*. A noble was worth 6*s*. 8*d*.

ACT I, SCENE III

1   *Good wives* other customers seeking to enter with
        Drugger; see I.iv.1–3.

5   *Free ... Grocers* i.e. admitted to the Grocers'
        Company, and thus a properly qualified tradesman.

9   *plot* plan.

11   *necromancy* magic.

14   *wished* recommended.

15   *planets* i.e. horoscopes.

24–7   *Sophisticate ... clouts* various methods of adulterating
        tobacco spoiled and dried by long shipment.
        clouts rags.

30–1   *maple ... juniper* equipment for shredding, lighting
        and smoking tobacco.

32   *goldsmith* usurer.

36   *clothing* livery.

37   *called ... scarlet* i.e. made sheriff.

40   *preserve ... it* i.e. pay the fine for refusing office,
        since his fortune will be made another way.

43   *amused* puzzled.

44   *metoposcopy* fortune-telling from the forehead and
        face.

52   *chiromanty* fortune-telling by the hand.

54–6   *Mercury ... Libra* If Libra were indeed the house of
        life, the horoscope would be governed by Venus, but
        Subtle substitutes Mercury, patron of businessmen (as
        well as thieves and alchemists), to appeal to Drugger's
        commercial instincts.

57   *balance* profit (playing on the zodiacal sign for Libra).

59   *Ormus* Hormuz, then a centre of the spice trade.

65–8   *Mathlai ... boxes* The resonant names of the spirits
        who will keep Drugger's stock from becoming fly-
        blown are culled from a learned necromantic treatise
        appended to Cornelius Agrippa's *De Occulta Philosophia*
        (1567).

69   *lodestone* magnet.

72	*a puppet ... vice* a doll worked by wires.
73	*fucus* a cosmetic.
79	*give a say* make an attempt.
84	*crown* a coin worth 5 shillings.
87	*portague* Portuguese gold coin worth between £3. 5*s*. and £4. 10*s*.
95	*ill-days* unlucky days.
102	*beech-coal* the best grade of charcoal.
	cor'sive corrosive.
104	*stuff* i.e. dupes.
107	*intelligence* information.

ACT I, SCENE IV

3	*Lambeth* a red-light district to the south of the Thames.
5	*Thorough the trunk* through the speaking-tube.
9	*shift* change (from captain's uniform into the smoky attire of Lungs).
10	*presently* at once.
14	*magisterium* (Lat.) master-work.
16	*possessed* a pun: (1) the owner; (2) mad.
20	*Reaching* offering.
	Moorfields an area of open ground outside the northern walls of London, laid out in walks in 1606.
21	*pomander-bracelets* aromatic protection against infection.
23	*spital* hospital.

ACT II, SCENE I

2	*novo orbe* (Lat). new world, America.
4	*Ophir* where Solomon was reputed to have made gold with the philosopher's stone, from which it was shipped every three years (see 1 Kings 9:28–10:23).
7	*happy ... 'Be rich'* see I.ii.119 n. cf. *The Faerie Queene*

II.vii.32. Jonson may intend an ironic echo of Spenser's Cave of Mammon episode.

8   *spectatissimi* (Lat.) most highly esteemed.

9   *hollow die* loaded dice (singular form).

10–14 *No more ... commodity* 'You shall no longer have the expense of employing a prostitute to persuade a young heir to sign a promissory note, nor, when he refuses to pay up, have him beaten until he does, just as he will beat the man who brings him the parcel of commodities he will be forced to contract for in order to pay his debt.' This refers to the commodity swindle, whereby the borrower of money was obliged to take his loan as a (grossly overvalued) parcel of goods which the usurer would buy back at a fraction of their cost.

16   *entrails* lining.

17   *Madam Augusta's* a brothel.

18   *sons ... hazard* fighters and gamblers.

19   *golden calf* an allusion to the idolatry of the Israelites (Exodus 32); and yet Mammon is the greatest gold-worshipper of them all.

22   *start up* beget.

23   *punketees* little punks (a nonce-word).

26   *fire-drake* fiery dragon, meteor; hence 'tender of the fire'.

27   *lungs* bellows-man.
        Zephyrus the west wind (in Greek mythology).

28   *firk* stir, excite.

29   *faithful* believing.

33   *Lothbury* a London street of copper-founders.

35–6 *Devonshire ... Indies* i.e. by turning their tin and copper into gold.

36   *admire* marvel.

49   *virtue* power.

55   *renew ... eagle* a blasphemy, since this is an activity of God (Exodus 19:5, Psalm 103:5, Isaiah 40:31).

56   *fifth age* old age.

57–8   *philosophers ... flood* Alchemists claimed that the biblical patriarchs possessed the elixir, which explained their longevity and the potency of Noah and Abraham, who begot children in old age.

60   *grain of mustard* another blasphemy, recalling Christ's words about the power of faith (Matthew 17:20).

61   *Marses ... Cupids* Cupid was son of Mars and Venus.

62   *vestals* virgin priestesses, here (facetiously) whores.
       Pict-hatch a notorious district of London.

63   *fire* (1) sexual passion; (2) venereal disease.

64   *nature naturized* the *natura naturata* of scholastic philosophy; the created world.

71   *players ... praises* i.e. because the plague closed the theatres.

73   *man* servant.

76   *waterwork* referring to recent and continuing improvements in London's water supply, for which charges were levied.

77   *humour* disposition (see Prologue, 9 n.).

78   *gulled* fooled, tricked.

79   *Pertinax* (Lat.) obstinate.

86   *the primitive tongue* the original language, spoken by Adam.

89   *Jason's fleece* Alchemists had indeed interpreted in this way the fleece sought by Jason in the Greek legend.

92   *Pythagoras' thigh* reputedly golden.
       Pandora's tub Pandora's box, from which all the ills of mankind had issued, had been reinterpreted as the philosopher's stone by the contemporary alchemist Delrio.

93–6   *Medea's ... teeth* Medea had restored the youth of Aeson; but Mammon is thinking mainly of her part in Jason's legendary quest for the golden fleece. She had cast a spell on the dragon guarding the fleece. Jason also had to yoke and plough with fire-breathing bulls in order to win the fleece. When Cadmus sowed dragon's teeth in Mars's field they sprang up as armed men: another of Jason's tasks was to sow the teeth unused by Cadmus, and Medea helped him defeat the warriors.

98   *Jason's helm*   The helmet punningly becomes a piece of alchemical apparatus (see Glossary).

101   *Hesperian garden*   of Greek mythology, where the golden apples grow, guarded by a dragon.

102   *Jove's shower*   Jove wooed Danae in a shower of gold.
boon of Midas   King Midas asked for, and was cursed by, the golden touch.
Argus   the hundred-eyed guardian of Io, charmed to sleep by Hermes.

103   *Boccace his Demogorgon*   described by Boccaccio (*De Genealogia Deorum*) as the primeval god, hence a synonym for the ultimate alchemical mystery.

ACT II, SCENE II

8   *Give ... affront*   look lords boldly in the eye.
14   *coverings*   roofing lead.
15   *bare*   i.e. bare-headed.
        auditory   congregation.
18   *manumit*   release.
23   *just*   exactly.
25   *several colours*   i.e. which denote the various stages of the process, and associated with animals and birds.
28   *sanguis agni*   (Lat, 'blood of the lamb') red, the final colour. The phrase has powerful religious overtones ('the saving blood of Christ').
43–4   *Tiberius ... Elephantis*   a reference to the depraved Roman emperor's collection of pornographic art.
44   *Aretine*   Aretino, Italian satirist (1492–1556), became known as a pornographer because of poems written for obscene pictures by Giulio Romano.
48   *succubae*   demons in female shape, hence 'whores'.
55   *sublimed*   pure (playing on the alchemical term).

62	*burgesses* members of parliament.
63	*the fart* A number of poems on this subject seem to have been current, though not finding their way into print until 1656.
64	*entertain* employ
67	*for them* as far as they are concerned.
74	*hyacinths* blue precious stones.
77	*Apicius* a Roman glutton.
79	*carbuncle* red precious stone.
80	*calvered* cut up alive.
81	*knots, godwits* edible birds.
	lampreys eel-like fish.
82	*barbels* fish of the carp species.
89	*taffeta-sarsnet* a fine silk fabric.
91	*the Persian* Sardanapalus, luxurious king of Nineveh (ninth century BC).
97	*homo frugi* (Lat.) a temperate man. (Piety and purity were thought to be moral prerequisites of alchemical success.)
101	*venture* investment.
105	*alone* only.

ACT II, SCENE III

1	*Father* Mammon and Subtle use the styles of Roman Catholic acolyte and priest, while Surly is treated as a heretic.
4	*doubt* fear.
5–6	*meet ... point* are very punctual.
	prevent anticipate.
8	*importune* importunate, untimely.
15	*ends* aims.
18	*prodigy* abnormality.
19	*prevaricate* deviate from the path.
21	*catholic* (1) universal, but (2) developing the Roman Catholic ecclesiastical language of the scene.

26   *costive* constipated, i.e. unwilling.
29   *bright ... robe* i.e. the essence of gold is ready.
30–1 *triple ... spirit* the vital, natural and animal spirits that linked the soul to the body.
32   *Ulenspiegel* Owlglass, trickster-hero of German jest books.
33   *Anon* straight away.
36   *D* The different parts of the apparatus are alphabetically labelled.
42   *next to canting* second only to thieves' jargon.
45   *lent* slow.
47   *is perfect* which is completed.
48   *covetise* Covetousness would prevent the projection.
51   *marrying* i.e. by providing dowries.
71   *The ... a-pitching* The rabbit-snare is set. Thieves' cant for confidence trickery was 'cony (i.e. rabbit) catching'.
80   *ferret* used to chase rabbits from the burrow.
81   *rank* smelly.
82   *Let ...die* Let the experiment lapse.
88   *bolted* i.e. like a rabbit from the ferret.
106–14 Each distillation increases the power of the elixir to transmute base metals.
116 *andirons* metal bars supporting a log fire.
119 *spits ... racks* instruments for cooking meat before a fire.
123–4 *faith ... hope ... charity* the three great spiritual virtues (see 1 Corinthians 13:13). Surly ridicules the quasi-religious tone of the proceedings.
128 *eggs in Egypt* i.e. by artificial incubation, as reported by Pliny.
131–76 Subtle's argument, that the alchemist in making gold simply speeds up nature's own striving towards perfection, is taken from Delrio's *Disquisitiones Magicae* (1599–1600).
157 *means* intermediate stages.
172–3 *Art ... creatures* i.e. that certain insects are generated

spontaneously by carrion (a belief founded in ignorance of the way in which insects laid their eggs).

174   *ritely*   (1) according to ritual, (2) with a pun on *rightly*, 'correctly'.

178   *bray*   pound. See Proverbs 27:21–26.

182   *charming*   casting of spells.

182–98 The alchemical terms listed by Surly, all taken from standard books on the subject, are explained in the Glossary.

194   *terms*   menses.

195   *clouts*   clods.

       merds   excrement.

198–207 Subtle rehearses a view, common among the alchemists, hermeticists and neo-Platonists of the Renaissance, that the obscurity of arcane writings protected mysteries from vulgar eyes.

203   *mystic symbols*   hieroglyphics (as yet undeciphered).

204   *Scriptures*   See Mark 4:12.

208   *cleared*   explained.

       Sisyphus   condemned in the Greek myth to the ceaseless rolling of a huge stone up a hill, as a punishment for revealing divine secrets.

210   *made ours common*   made our alchemical secrets generally known. Mammon's unconsciously ironic use of Doll's surname cues her entry.

217   *still*   always.

223   *I warrant*   I will protect.

225   *Bradamante*   an Amazon (female warrior) in Ariosto's *Orlando Furioso* (1532). Hence *brave*: (1) warlike; (2) finely dressed.

226   *burnt*   i.e. as a heretic. Surly sustains his ridicule of Mammon's 'faith'.

230–1 *Paracelsian … physic*   i.e. a follower of Paracelsius (1493–1541), who applied alchemical principles in medicine (*mineral physic*).

233   *Galen*   physician (AD 130–210), identified with traditional medicine.

235   *This*   i.e. Surly.
238   *Broughton*   Hugh Broughton (1549–1612), Puritan divine and rabbinical scholar.
241   *genealogies*   See IV.v.1–32 n.
244   *divers*   various men.
       upon the conference   obscure: perhaps 'over the question of how to meet her'.
256   *vegetal*   playing on Lat. *vegetus*, 'active', 'lively' (see Glossary).
260   *Ulen!*   The Folio text includes this in Mammon's previous speech. Gifford's emendation seems preferable.
268   *original*   origin.
282   *And*   if.
284   *trick*   (1) hand at cards; (2) card-sharping.
284–5 *primero ... gleek*   card games.
287–8 *quicksilver ... sulphur*   (1) remedies for venereal diseases; (2) basic alchemical materials.
288   *one*   someone.
289   *Temple church*   a church amidst the legal chambers of the Temple, and thus a convenient place for business appointments.
295   *see her converse*   an obvious euphemism.
297   *by attorney*   i.e. in disguise.
303   *quainter traffickers*   more cunning traders, i.e. pimps, with a pun on *quaint*, 'female pudenda'.
304   *visitor*   official inspector.
306   *fall*   a flat collar.
       tire   dress.
307   *prove*   test.
315   *parlous head*   dangerous (i.e. sharp) mind.
320   *Bantam*   in Java, a place of fabulous riches.
324–6 *jack ... weights*   mechanism that turned a roasting spit.
329   *chain*   badge of office.
330   *vermin*   playing on the *ermine* of the judge's robe.
331   *Count Palatine*   having jurisdiction over the Counties Palatine, Cheshire and Lancashire.

ACT II, SCENE IV

1   *bit* Fishing is a persistent analogy in this scene.

5   *firks mad* jerks about (with an obscene innuendo).

7   *statelich* (Dutch) in a stately manner.

8   *race* breeding.

11   *woman* servant.

     Sanguine the amorous, optimistic humour.

17   *angle* fishing-tackle.

18   *gudgeons* fish that will swallow anything.

20   *Anabaptist* belonging to a religious sect of German origin which appeared in England in the 1530s. They advocated primitive Christianity, adult baptism and common ownership, and refused civil oaths, aiming to set up a theocracy. They were regarded as seditious.

21   *gold-end man* dealer in scrap precious metals.

30   *Amsterdam* one of the Dutch towns in which the Anabaptists had attempted to gain control during the 1590s. Their failure led to persecution and exile.

31   *raise ... discipline* advance their sect.

ACT II, SCENE V

7   *brother* Ananias intends 'Puritan', but Subtle deliberately misunderstands him to mean 'fellow alchemist'.

8   *Lullianist ... Ripley* The alchemical works attributed (probably wrongly) to Raymond Lull (or Lully) (1235–1315), Spanish courtier and missionary to the Arabs, were popularized in England by George Ripley (?d. 1490), Canon of Bridlington.

8   *Filius artis* (Lat., 'son of art') alchemist.

11   *homogene ... heterogene* of one kind ... of several kinds.

13   *Knipper-Doling* Bernt Knipperdollink was one of the leaders of the Anabaptist rising at Münster in 1534–6, under John of Leyden.

     Ars sacra (Lat., 'sacred art') alchemy.

15   *pamphysic ... panarchic* Jonsonian nonce-words: of all nature ... of all power (from the Greek).

17   *All ... Hebrew* because Hebrew was (1) the language
        of the Old Testament and (2) reputed to be the
        language spoken by Adam in paradise (cf. Mammon,
        II.i.84–6 and note). The more extreme Puritans
        rejected secular and classical learning.

20   *vexations ... martyrizations* chemical changes. The
        religious ring of these terms is not unusual in
        alchemical language, and here calculated to arouse
        Ananias.

28   *trine ... spheres* (1) Alchemical processes were
        frequently linked to astrology. Here the *trine circle*
        indicates a favourable conjunction of planets in the
        seven spheres ranked below the *firmament* (see Glossary).
        (2) A sevenfold process has to be repeated three times.

34   *suscitability* excitability.

37–9   *shifting ... dry* i.e. shifting the elements through the
        four basic qualities ascribed to matter in Aristotelian
        physics, in order to achieve the perfect balance of such
        qualities, which was the property of gold.

57   *Sincere professors* convinced Anabaptists.

71   *pin-dust* metal filings from the manufacture of pins.

72–3   *Ananias ... Apostles* See Acts 5:1–10, where Ananias
        and his wife fall dead when Peter denounces them for
        keeping money from the Apostles.

74   *consistory* religious assembly.

77–8   *make atonement ... satisfaction* The theological langu-
        age here, casting Surly in the role of wrathful god,
        parodies the Anabaptists' religious beliefs.

82–3   *bishops ... hierarchy* The episcopacy of the English
        church was hated by the Puritans as a relic of popery.

90   *froward* perverse, ungovernable.

ACT II, SCENE VI

2   *mates* low company.
        Bayards horses (a jocular reference to the magic horse
        given by Charlemagne to Rinaldo), with a suggestion

of foolishness, as in the proverb 'bold as blind Bayard'.

11   *balance*   the constellation of Libra.

11–18   Subtle makes the rebus not with conventional astrological signs (*Taurus, Aries*), but with an iconography that is *mystic* (i.e. 'of mysterious power'), the *radii* ('rays') of which will have a *virtual influence* ('influence due to its power') on the *affections* ('inclinations') of passers-by.

18   *result upon*   benefit.

20   *Dee*   Dr John Dee (1527–1608), mathematician, astrologer and occultist.

22   *anenst*   opposite.

24   *hieroglyphic*   The occult sciences of the Renaissance were dominated by hermeticism, thought to have originated in Egypt.

26   *legs*   bows.

30   *bona roba*   (Lat., 'good robe') tart, prostitute (slang).

32–3   *fashion ... a-cop*   Hats were in fashion, but provincial Dame Pliant wears a French hood on the top of her head.

34–5   *fucus ... deal*   The *double entendre* on *fucus* is reinforced by the play on *deal*, (1) sell, (2) copulate.

36   *physic*   medicines.

38   *match*   i.e. as stupid as Drugger.

42–3   *it ... marriage*   that gossip about it will reduce her marriage prospects.

54   *o' the city dubbed*   merchants knighted.

55   *water*   either (1) a love-potion or (2) a sample of urine for analysis.

57   *newly warm in*   having recently inherited.

64   *by line*   accurately.

66   *table*   diagram.

69   *instrument*   document.

71   *happ'ly*   (1) perhaps; (2) happily, favourably.

73   *premises*   prospects.

84   *This works*   This is going well.

85   *on*   of.

87   *in tail*   punning on (1) the legal term to describe

restricted inheritance of an estate and (2) sexual slang
(*tail*, 'pudendum').

88   *light*   wanton (but introducing a play on 'weight').
89   *grains*   weight (to compensate for the loss in goods).
89–90   *burden ... whole*   The sexual innuendo continues.

ACT III, SCENE I

2   *separation*   (1) exile; (2) elect of God, separated as
         sheep from goats (Matthew 25:32–3).
6   *of Canaan*   i.e. of the infidel (see Isaiah 19:18).
8   *mark ... Beast*   i.e. of the damned (see Revelation
         16:2, 19:20).
11   *bend*   conform.
17   *give*   concede.
22   *choleric*   prone to anger.
32   *beauteous discipline*   i.e. Puritanism.
33   *menstruous ... Rome*   The Roman priest's surplice and
         the Scarlet Woman of Revelation 18 are linked by this
         Puritan cant phrase.
36   *weighing*   considering.
38   *silenced saints*   (1) suppressed Anabaptists; (2) (perhaps
         also) Puritan clergy excommunicated by the Hampton
         Court conference in 1604.
41   *aurum potabile*   (Lat., 'drinkable gold') bribery (playing
         on the alchemical sense of 'sovereign remedy').
48   *motion*   impulse.
49   *spirit*   the Holy Spirit, third person of the Trinity,
         comforter and counsellor of the believer (John 16:7–
         15).

ACT III, SCENE II

10   *doth qualify*   moderates my indignation (playing on the
         alchemical term). See also ll. 14, 18.
17   *numbered*   included.
22   *main*   main use.

23   *Hollanders* The Dutch navy, employed mainly in the defence of the East India trade, was large and powerful. Subtle suggests that it could be hired as a mercenary force in the cause of an English Anabaptist theocracy.

25   *make ... faction* win you support.

27   *in state* in high office.

33–4   *past ... mind* i.e. physically incapable of sex, though mentally still disposed to it.

36   *oil of talc* (1) a cosmetic face wash; (2) the alchemist's white elixir.

37–8   *leper ... bone-ache* referring ostensibly to (1) skin disease and arthritis, but probably intending (2) the symptoms of syphilis.

40   *fricace* embrocation.

41   *pregnant* convincing.

43   *plate* gold and silver dishes.
        Christ-tide avoiding the popish word 'mass'.

44   *Yet* still. (Subtle continues to insist upon a restraint that Ananias finds impossible.)

45   *parcel gilt* partly gilded silver.
        massy solid (but does Subtle intend a pun on the popish mass, slyly mocking Ananias?).

50   *lords ... temporal* governors of church and state.

51   *oppone* oppose.

54   *exercises* sermons or extempore prayers.

55–60   *'ha' ... bell* Subtle suggests that the mannerisms of Puritan preaching and devotion could be arranged as a tune, a means of calling the faithful together as effective as church bells.

56–8   *such ... together,* those politically dispossessed are justified in exploiting religious discontents in order to form a faction.

61   *Bells are profane* because they are another 'popish' feature of the established church.

63   *it shall down* the apparatus shall be destroyed (if Ananias continues his zealous interjections).

64–5   *all ... grace* see II.v. 77–8n.

66–8   *neither ... need* he simply agreed with you in

occasionally permitting tunes, and we shall no longer need them, having the stone.

to'ard   toward, close to achieving.

69–82 This is a conventional catalogue of Puritan hypocrisies.

69   *vizard*   mask; hence facial expression.

72   *start*   advantage.

77   *stiffness*   stubborn pride, with a sexual innuendo that may relate to accusations that Puritan sects indulged in orgies.

78   *scrupulous bones*   meticulous but trivial doctrinal issues.

79–82 Puritans opposed such practices.

87   *shorten ... ears*   Several notable Puritans had had their ears cropped, the usual punishment for sedition.

88   *wire-drawn grace*   an excruciatingly extended prayer before a meal.

89   *please ... alderman*   Puritan sympathizers among the London city fathers opposed the theatres.

95   *wood*   collection, crowd (Lat. *silva*).

102   *idle to it*   empty in comparison with it.

102–6 This is a summary, in typically mystical language, of the occult Renaissance philosophy (of which alchemy was a part) that sought power over the spirits and angels controlling the workings of nature, and which originated among the Arabs, Jews, Greeks and Egyptians (hence *From east to west*).

106   *traditions*   The Puritans rejected as popish any religious practice not grounded in the Bible and personal revelation.

113   *botcher*   a tailor who does repairs.

       revelation   i.e. divine revelation. The Puritans identified with the Apostles – simple, uneducated men who were enlightened directly by Christ and the Holy Spirit.

126   *expect*   wait.

131–2 *second ... month*   i.e. 16 November 1610, which places the action of the play on 1 November; but at V.v.102–3 Ananias seems to suggest 23 October as the play's date. Here Ananias scrupulously avoids the heathen names of the months.

134   *hundred marks*   £66. 13*s*. 4*d*.

140   *lenter*   slower.

144   *tincture*   not in the alchemical sense, but meaning simply a change of colour.
         Dutch dollars   silver coins worth about 5 English shillings.

146   *bide … examination*   withstand any official test.

150   *know no magistrate*   i.e. defy the civil authority in matters of conscience.

151   *foreign coin*   Counterfeiting foreign coin was in fact a treasonable offence in English law.

151–2   *coining … casting*   Such casuistry was a common target of anti-Puritan satire.

ACT III, SCENE III

2   *came on*   turned up.
         walked the round   (1) kept lookout; (2) referring to the circular Temple church where Face was to have met Surly.

3   *quit him*   given him up.

4   *hell … too*   Face angrily suggests the other sense of *quit*, 'requite'.

5   *mill-jade*   horse harnessed to a mill, walking in a circle.

6   *grains*   (1) money; (2) continuing the mill simile.

8   *black*   sooty.

11   *compeer*   partner.
         party-bawd   (1) partner in bawdry; (2) part-time pimp.

12   *conscience*   religious convictions. (Is the Don a Protestant?)

13–19   Face sees the Don as a new Armada, come to invade England in the person of Doll.

13   *munition*   provisions.
         slops   baggy trousers.

14   *hoys*   small sailing vessels.

       trunks   padded breeches.

15   *pistolets*   Spanish gold coins, worth about 17 shillings.

       pieces of eight   Spanish dollars, worth between 4 and 5 shillings.

16   *bath*   common euphemism for brothel.

17   *colour*   pretext.

18   *Cinque Port*   one of the fortified ports, Dover among them, on the south coast of England.

21   *in chief*   especially.

22   *epididymis*   duct leading from the testicles.

23   *doxy*   low woman.

24   *John Leydens*   i.e. Ananias and Tribulation, after John of Leyden, Anabaptist leader at Munster (1534–6).

29   *reversions*   promised future benefits (legal).

30   *states*   estates, property.

33   *Say ... camp*   the opening line of Kyd's *Spanish Tragedy* (*c.* 1587; one of the great popular successes of the Elizabethan theatre), ushering in another military simile.

41   *dousabel*   sweet and beautiful (Fr. *douce et belle*).

44   *drum*   (1) probably 'belly'; (2) continuing the military metaphor.

46   *the great frost*   from December 1607 to February 1608.

47   *bees ... basin*   Banging on a hollow utensil was said to induce a swarm to settle.

49   *God's gift*   the Greek meaning of Dorothea.

50   *adalantado*   (Sp.) governor, grandee.

53   *a-furnishing*   getting their money together.

54   *Would*   i.e. should.

57   *chapman*   merchant.

       'em   Mammon's household metalwork.

58   *against*   in anticipation that.

64   *conjuring ... circle*   (1) Spirits were raised within a magic circle; (2) another reference to the round Temple church.

67   *virginal*   a keyboard instrument (with a *double entendre*).

70   *mother-tongue* Face plays wittily on kissing and speaking.
71   *Verdugoship* a comic title derived from Spanish *verdugo*, 'executioner'.
       language English.
73   *obscure* secretly.
78   *tire* costume.
82   *angry boy* young man cultivating a fashionable quarrelsomeness.

ACT III, SCENE IV

10   *Kastril* named after a hawk (kestrel).
12   *as he likes* when he says so.
13   *'Good time* All in good time.
14   *sorry else* poorer otherwise.
18   *carry a business* organize a duel.
22   *take tobacco* a new and extremely fashionable pastime.
25   *practise* i.e. behave as a gallant.
28   *instrument* (1) a document or treatise; (2) (metaphorically) a scientific instrument, in keeping with the geometrical language of Face's description of the art of duelling (ll.30–40).
37   *To give ... by* to exchange accusations of lying (pretexts for duelling).
40-1   *ordinarily ... academies* a pun on *ordinary*, 'eating-house'.
43   *You ... reads it* You cannot imagine any technicality he is unable to understand (with a pun on Subtle's name).
47   *enter* introduce.
50   *spend* financially ruin.
52   *vented* spent.
61   *groom-porter's* Lord Chamberlain's officer supervising games of cards, dice and bowls at court.
68   *dainty* i.e. woman.
70   *poet* playwright.

71   *affects*   desires.

76   *cast*   cashiered.

79   *by* ... *posts*   with the speed of post-horses.

81   *punk* ... *boy*   whore and catamite.

87   *perspective*   (1) a picture or diagram; (2) a glass or
        mirror (see I.i.97).

90   *commodity*   See II.i.10–14 n.

105   *suster*   sister, in Kastril's rural dialect.

108   *pass it*   let it pass.

119   *Seacoal Lane*   a London street, running from Snow
        Hill to Fleet Lane.

120   *sodden*   boiled.
        pellitory o' the wall   a medicinal herb.

123   *'sessed*   assessed for charges.

124   *waterwork*   See II.i.76 n.

125   *Thy* ... *off*   proverbially a symptom of venereal
        disease. Is Face hinting that this, and not the price of
        water, was the cause of Drugger's baldness?

138–9   *do* ... *worship*   bring you more credit.

143   *old* ... *sovereign*   worth only 10 shillings at this time.

144   *groat*   worth 4*d*.

145   *twenty nobles*   £6. 13*s*. 4*d*., an accurate total of the
        coins specified.
        just   exact (with a hint at Dapper's parsimoniousness).

146–7   *Maries* ... *Maries*   coins from Queen Mary's reign,
        to complete the numismatic sequence of Dapper's
        gratuities.

ACT III, SCENE V

SD   *Priest of Fairy*   The Court of Chancery (1609–10) was
        told that one Thomas Rogers was successfully gulled in
        this way.

5–18   Subtle, as Priest of Fairy, speaks a clumsily rhyming
        verse to create an atmosphere of spurious enchantment
        that would appeal to the naïve Dapper.

10   *nearer* ... *smock*   a proverbial saying, given an

indecent edge by the association with Fortune, proverbially a whore (see *Hamlet* II.ii.236 ff.).

12   *being*   when he was.

        rent   torn.

15   *eyes ... fortunate*   because Fortune too is blind.

15 SD   *rag*   suggests the contrast between illusion and reality
        in the scene's enchantments.

17   *pelf*   wealth.

27   *Directly*   honestly.

30   *transitory*   i.e. worldly.

31 SD   *cithern*   a guitar-like instrument.

33   *spur-rial*   Edward IV noble, worth about 15 shillings.

40   *innocent*   (1) guiltless person; (2) simpleton.

55   *puffin*   (1) comical seabird, thought to be half fish; (2)
        perhaps also 'puffed up'.

56   *o' the spit ... back*   Dapper, like roasting meat, must
        be temporarily kept warm at the back of the fire.

74   *stay*   gag.

76   *crinkle*   shrink from his purpose.

ACT IV, SCENE I

8   *in her fit*   This phrase, used of Doll's impatience to see
        Mammon, ominously suggests the madness induced
        by religious controversy against which Face forewarns
        him.

16   *state*   politics.

18   *controversy*   i.e. religious disputes.

19   *house*   noble family.

23   *modern happiness*   (1) commonplace or trite enjoyment;
        (2) contemporary aptness (facetious).

25   *Heighten*   in the alchemical sense of 'strengthen,
        purify'.

26–7   *Jove ... Danae*   See II.i.102.

30   *concumbere*   (Lat.) copulate.

38   *Guinea-bird*   prostitute (slang).

44   *gat*   begot.

51   *seeds ... materials* Doll uses an alchemical metaphor
        to describe the remnants of her supposed family's
        nobility. Mammon continues it, ll. 51–3.

56   *Austriac* i.e. the Habsburgs, famed for their full lower
        lip.

57   *costermonger* apple-seller.

58   *Valois* kings of France.

59   *Medici* rulers of Florence.

69   *Phoenix* legendary bird, said to die in flames and rise
        from its own ashes.

70   *court* seek to be.

71   *art* artifice.

75   *feature* physique.

78   *Particular* Doll takes Mammon to be suggesting
        physical intimacy.

83   *mathematics* astrology.

84   *distillation* chemistry.

90   *Kelly* Edward Kelly (1555–95), associate of John Dee.
        He interested the Emperor Rudolf II in his alchemical
        prowess, the failure of which led to imprisonment at
        Prague.

92   *Aesculapius* the great physician of classical mytho-
        logy, killed by Zeus with a thunderbolt, lest he should
        make man immortal.

101   *a mere solecism* completely inappropriate.

118   *styles* titles of nobility.

119   *jealousy* suspicion.

122   *the mastery* the stone.

126   *shower* See II.i.102.

134   *hundred* subdivision of a county.

136   *emp'rics* (1) ancient physicians who based their
        remedies on experience, not theory; (2) possibly
        'quacks'.

145   *Poppaea* Nero's beautiful, luxurious and notorious
        second wife.

153   *in ... prison* because of the monarch's jealousy or, as
        in Kelly's case, impatience.

156   *free state* republic.

174   *Rabbins*   rabbis, Hebrew scholars, whose controversies would throw Doll into her fit.

ACT IV, SCENE II

5   *bonnibel*   pretty girl (Fr. *bonne et belle*).
6   *suit*   his captain's uniform.
7   *curtain*   perhaps a drop-scene in a masque, effecting a sudden transformation.
9   *hit ... nostrils*   lead you by the nose.
13   *terrae fili*   (Lat. 'son of earth') (1) base person; (2) in alchemy, spirit; (3) Face mockingly intends 'land-owner'.
15   *lusts*   desires, not necessarily sexual.
17   *Charge*   attack.
20   *sudden*   impetuous.
21   *aforehand*   i.e. the initiator of the quarrel.
21–8   Subtle applies the language of scholastic logic to duelling, as Face had previously used geometrical terms (III.iv.30–40).
40   *subtlety*   (1) a sugar confection; (2) delicacy.
42   *myrobalane*   a plum-like fruit.
43   *In rivo frontis*   (Lat.) on the frontal vein.
45   *linea Fortunae*   (Lat.) line of Fortune (from the base of the little finger to the index).
46   *stella ... Veneris*   (Lat.) star on the Hill of Venus (at the base of the thumb).
47   *junctura annularis*   (Lat.) the joint of the ring-finger.
48   *soldier ... art*   i.e. Face or Subtle.
53   *kuss*   kiss, in Kastril's rustic dialect.
59   *fustian*   bogus.
       dark glass   the fortune-teller's crystal ball.
60   *dabchick*   the little grebe, a small, delicate bird.
64–5   *grammar ... rhetoric*   i.e. the complete scheme of study.
67   *several*   variable.
71   *Against*   (1) until; (2) in preparation for when.

3   *composition*   (1) agreement; (2) compensation.

10   *serve*   the farmyard (sexual) sense is included.

20   *Don John*   stock name for a Spaniard.

21   'Gentlemen, I kiss your honours' hands.'

26   *collar of brawn*   pig's neck.

27   *souse*   ear.
         wriggled   cut into patterns resembling the folds in a
         ruff.

30   *D'Alva*   governor of the Netherlands, 1567–73.
         Egmont   Flemish patriot executed by D'Alva in 1568.

32   *Gracias*   Thanks.

33   *squibs*   explosive charges.
         sets   the pleats of Surly's ruff, seen as trenches or
         crenellations in a fortification.

34   'By God, gentlemen, a most charming house.'

36   *action*   gestures.

40   *Donzel*   little Don.
         Entiendo   I understand (though Face and Subtle do not
         realize this).

44–5   *pumpèd ... Dry*   i.e. sexually as well as financially.

46   *See all ... of all*   obscure: perhaps (1) see all the rare
         shows and sights of the town; (2) be given the
         runaround.

47   'If you please, may one see this lady?'

52   *stay*   wait.

60   *sudden*   quick.

61–2   'I understand that the lady is so beautiful that I long to
         see her as the great good fortune of my life.'

67   *which on's*   whichever of us.

70   *house*   business.
         engaged   involved.

73   *doom*   judgement, decision.

74–5   *win ... wear her*   a phrase proverbially used of court-
         ship, given a coarse meaning here.

75   *work her*   (1) persuade her (to lie with Surly); (2) make
         her work (as a prostitute).

78   'Gentlemen, why so much delay?'
80   'Perhaps you are mocking my love.'
82   *loose the hinges* either (1) tell all, or (2) break our partnership.
84   *think of* remember.
87   *Hands* Shake hands.
91   *por ... barbas* 'By this honoured beard'
93   'I fear, gentlemen, that you are practising some treachery on me.'
94–6   Subtle uses mock-Spanish.
98   *fubbed* cheated.
100   *curried* like leather, beaten and scraped in its preparation.
        flawed flayed.
        tawed (1) softened with alum, like leather; (2) beaten.

ACT IV, SCENE IV

1   *leave* give up.
2   *nick* critical point.
7   *inns-of-court-man* lawyer.
9   *jennet* small Spanish horse.
10   *Stoop* bow.
        garb fashion.
12   *pavan* a stately dance.
13   *titillation* perfume.
18   *scheme* horoscope.
        undergo a sexual pun.
26   *rests* remains.
29   *eighty-eight* 1588, year of the Armada. Dame Pliant is thus aged 19 in 1610.
32   *rush* Rushes were strewn on the floor.
33   *cry strawberries* become a (poor) fruitseller.
34   *shads* herring.
41   *ruffled* fondled.
        hangings cloth wall-hangings.
42   *know her state* be aware of her status.

43   *idolators ... chamber* sycophantic courtiers.

44   *Barer* i.e. with heads uncovered, as a mark of respect.

47   *th'Exchange* the New Exchange in the Strand, a fashionable shopping centre.

48   *Bedlam* Bethlehem Hospital was a madhouse. Spectators paid to watch the inmates' antics.
      China-houses shops selling oriental goods.

50   *goose-turd bands* collars of a fashionable yellowish green.

53–4 'Why is it, gentlemen, that she doesn't come? This delay is killing me.'

56   Subtle's mock-Spanish: 'A fine lady, Don, very fine!'

57–8 'By all the gods, the most perfect beauty I have seen in my life!'

61   *law-French* forensic jargon, derived from Norman French.

63–4 'The sun has lost his light, with the splendour that this lady brings. God bless me!'

69   'Why does she not come?'

71   'For the love of God, what is the matter, that she tarries?'

76–7 'My lady, my person is quite unworthy to approach such beauty.'

80   'Lady, if it is convenient, let us go in.'

83   *the word* i.e. to begin her 'fit'.

92   *erection ... figure* (1) casting of her horoscope; (2) perhaps a sexual innuendo.

ACT IV, SCENE V

1–32 Doll's ravings are based on Hugh Broughton's *A Concent of Scripture* (1590), a Puritan work of biblical chronology, and they principally concern Alexander's empire, which was taken by commentators to be one of the 'four kingdoms' mentioned in Daniel's interpretation of Nebuchadnezzar's dream (Daniel 2).

2–3	*Perdicas ... Ptolemy* the four generals who divided up and fought over Alexander's empire.
10	*fourth chain* the fourth period in Broughton's chronology.
16	*Eber, and Javan* i.e. Hebrew and Gentile.
19–20	*ancient ... consonants* the primeval language, key to all learning.
21	*Pythagoras* Greek philosopher, revered as magus by Renaissance occultists.
24	*lay* (1) subdue; (2) copulate with.
25	*Talmud* the corpus of Jewish civil and religious law.
26	*fifth monarchy* the millennium, Christ's 1000-year reign on earth. But Mammon dreams of a sensual and material triumph, not a spiritual one.
28	*Thogarma* royal house mentioned in Ezekiel 38:6. *Habergions* coats of mail.
31–2	*David Kimchi ... Ezra* biblical scholars.
34	*Close* secret.
41	*managing* going on.
58	*in fumo* in smoke.
62	*shivers* pieces.
86	*box* for charitable donations to the asylum.
103	*case* disguise (as Lungs).
107	*fetch him over* get the better of him.

ACT IV, SCENE VI

3	*clap* (1) blow; (2) gonorrhoea.
5	*punctually forward* ready to take advantage.
20–1	*melancholic ... coitum* sad after your sexual intercourse (*omne animal post coitum triste est*).
23	*upsee Dutch* Dutch fashion (Dutch *op zijn*).
24	*lumpish* stupidly dull.
29–30	*cart ... whip* Criminals were sometimes whipped through the streets behind a cart.
33	*parcel-broker* (1) part-time intermediary or go-

between; (2) pimp (hence *whole bawd*); (3) swindler
(hence *all rascal*).

38   *touch* A touchstone was used to test gold. Face's trick
with sulphur made the gold of his victims seem
worthless.

42-5   The client's gold (palmed by the alchemist) would
apparently be lost when the substituted flask of
mercury sublimate 'accidentally' exploded.

46   *Faustus* the eponymous protagonist of Marlowe's
play (1588?), a conjuror of spirits who sold his soul to
the devil in exchange for twenty-four years of knowledge and power.

48   *ephemerides* astronomical almanacs.

49   *holds intelligence* exchanges information.

51   *damsels with child* Subtle is either (1) offering a
pregnancy-testing service or (2) procuring abortions –
perhaps both.

53   *green-sickness* chlorosis, an anaemia afflicting pube-
scent girls.

54   *answer ... ears* See I.i.169 n. and III.ii.87 n.

ACT IV, SCENE VII

16   *foist* (1) pickpocket; (2) rogue.

17   *had him presently* saw through him immediately.

21   *temptation ... spirit* See above, ll.8–11.

23   *mauther* wench (Norfolk dialect).

25   *swabber* common seaman (used contemptuously).

26   *out of company* because you are not alone.

31   *on* from.

32   *And ... me* And he has been swearing false oaths to
pay me for a year.

33   *lotium* stale urine, used in hairdressing.

34   *syringes* perhaps for applying lotium (obscure).
Hydra many-headed mythological monster.

39   *trig* dandy, coxcomb.

40   *Amadis ... Quixote* eponymous heroes of popular romances, a genre held in low esteem by Jonson.

41   *Knight ... Coxcomb* (1) because Surly wears an extravagant hat; (2) alluding to Beaumont and Fletcher's play *The Coxcomb*, based on *The Curious Impertinent* from *Don Quixote*.

45–6 *otter ... tim* Kastril's insults are obscure in their meaning, but obviously rather feeble.

50   *Avoid* go away.

53   *unclean ... seventy-seven* *unclean birds* echoes Revelation 18:2; a pamphlet of 1586 mentions birds with ruffs caught in Lincolnshire.

54   *prank it with* swagger.

55   *Antichrist* Christ's great antagonist, to be defeated in the millennium, whom Ananias would identify with the Pope.

56–7 *take ... course* fight.

60   *I ... to't* I shall succeed.

63   *prevented* anticipated.

66   *brokerly* See IV.vi.33 n.

68   *players* actors.

69   *did ... fool* Robert Armin, who created the part of Drugger, specialized in clown and comic roles for the King's Men.

71   *Hieronimo* protagonist of Kyd's *Spanish Tragedy*.

81–2 *locked ... out* as Edward II had done to Raymond Lull, and Queen Elizabeth to Cornelius Lannoy (in 1566).

90   *presently* at once.

92   *conceive* understand.

96   *looked* expected.

103   *honest* chaste.

      stand (1) bid for her hand; (2) with a sexual innuendo.

110   *quiblins* games.

114   *taken* caught.

116   *died* i.e. of the plague.

      liberties suburbs.

117   *walls* the city walls.

122   *purchase* winnings.

125   *Ratcliff* in Stepney, on the river Thames.

132–3   *shave* . . . *trim* playing on the secondary sense of
        'cheat'.

ACT V, SCENE I

6   *Pimlico* not the modern London district, but a house
        at Hoxton (see V.ii.19 n.) noted for its pies and ale.

11   *teaching* . . . *nose* puritanical preaching.

21   *ging* gang, crowd.

22   *motion* puppet-show.

31   *made away* murdered.

ACT V, SCENE II

19   *threaves* i.e. droves.
        Hogsden now Hoxton, in the Shoreditch district of
        London; then a semi-rural place of popular resort on
        the northern outskirts of the city (see V.i.6 n.).

20   *Eye-bright* perhaps an inn at Hoxton (obscure).

22   *one* . . . *hood* Dame Pliant (see II.vi.32–3).

23–4   *another* . . . *gown* Doll (see V.iv.134).

32   *black-pot* beer-mug.

44   *changelings* (1) people who change their minds easily;
        (2) idiots; (3) a cue to Neighbours 4, 5 and 6 to exit and
        change, if, as seems possible, they doubled as Kastril,
        Ananias and Tribulation. Ananias the botcher perhaps
        doubled as Neighbour 6, the stocking repairer.

ACT V, SCENE III

2   *mere* absolute.
        chancel eastern end of a church, leading to the
        sanctuary.

17   *lights* butcher's name for lungs.

22   *sign* suggesting that Surly had been at a tavern, ordinary or (most likely) a brothel, all of which displayed signs.

34   *cockatrice* a mythological monster; here, slang for 'whore'.

41   *fat ... gentleman* i.e. Mammon and Surly.

44   *seed ... fire* Ananias now links, through the brimstone common to both, alchemy and hell.

47   *unclean birds.* See IV.vii.53 n.

48   *scavenger* in charge of street-cleaning.

50   *Punk-device* arrant whore; playing on *point-device*, 'meticulous in dress'.

55   *St Kather'ne's* a hospital.

62   *deceptio visus* (Lat.) optical illusion.

67   *sets ... throat* raises his voice.

69   *Peace* silence.

78   *med'cine* charm, spell.

79   *draw* decoy, attract.

    wild-fowl geese (i.e. fools).

87   *'Tis but* it only requires.

89   *visited* i.e. by the plague.

ACT V, SCENE IV

7   *Captain* Dapper recognizes 'Captain' Face, despite his 'smooth' shaven appearance as Jeremy. Would this inconsistency in the conventional impenetrability of stage disguise pass unnoticed in the speed of the action?

8   *Is ... down* Is his gag gone?

11   *churl* countryman (Lovewit has been at his hopyards).

14   *coil* disturbance.

15   *dwindled* shrank (with fear).

18   *suit* petition.

33   *kind* natural, sincere.

34   *bird* familiar spirit, or 'fly'.

36   *this day se'night* in a week's time.

40   *come on* are born of.

41–2   *Woolsack ... Dagger* well-known London taverns.

42   *frumety* wheat boiled in milk and seasoned.

43   *Heaven and Hell* Westminster taverns.

44   *mumchance, tray-trip* dice games.

45   *God-make-you-rich* a variety of backgammon.

47   *Gleek and primero* See II.iii.284–5 n.

50   *and* if.

51   *learn* teach.

58   *your ... year* i.e. your estate.

60   *writings* legal documents.

62   *suit* the Spanish costume borrowed from the players.

64   *spend* earn, and so have to spend.

67   *innocent* See III.v.40 n.

72   *fit him* echoing a famous line from *The Spanish Tragedy* ('Why then, I'll fit you'), a costume from which has just been brought on stage.
        fit match.

77   *Brainford* now Brentford.

81   *instrument* agreement.

88   *flitter-mouse* bat, 'fly-by-night'.

89   *tickle it* enjoy ourselves.
        Pigeons a Brentford inn.

100   *bestow* position.

114   *single money* small change.

116   *and* if.
        Ward a famous Mediterranean pirate.

120   *bolts of lawn* rolls of fine linen.

126   *smock-rampant* Face conjurs a mock-heraldic device, based on Doll's main working garment.
        right truth.

128   *for ... figures* in spite of all your horoscopes.

129   *I ... him* not true; Face is rationalizing.

131   *Determines* ends.

133   *back-side* rear of the house.

136 *dock* criminal court.

140 *go hard* be difficult.

141 *letter* recommendation.

141–2 *Mistress* ... *Caesarean* brothel-keepers.

148 *i' the flock-bed* ... *buttery* i.e. while you eat and sleep.

ACT V, SCENE V

5 *for failing* in case we fail.

9 *ding* batter.

11 *collier* See I.i.90 n.

12 *birding* hunting, hence 'stealing'.

13 *Madam Suppository* (1) alluding to Doll's pretended study of medicine; (2) impostor ('supposed'); (3) whore.

14 *Bel* ... *Dragon* heathen idols (in the Apocrypha).

15 *grasshoppers* ... *lice* two of the plagues of Egypt (Exodus 8, 10).

20 *nun* whore (facetious).
    Madam Rabbi i.e. Doll in her fit (IV.v.1–32).

23 *staff* staff of office.

24 *cart* See IV.vi.29–30.

41 *poesies* ... *candle* graffiti written in candle-smoke.

42 *madam* ... *dildo* an obscene drawing (*dildo*, 'phallus').

48 *gone through* i.e. with the marriage.

56 *harquebusier* musketeer (armed with an harquebus).

59 *choughs* birds of the crow family.

60 *daws* jackdaws, with a reputation for stealing bright objects.

67 *public means* the lawcourts.

79 *younkers* youths.

80 *tits* ... *tomboys* young girls.

85 *hearken* seek.

100 *seal* mark of divine election and protection; see Revelation 7:3, 9:4.

103 *table dormant* a permanent side-table (the phrase has a ring that anticipates *The Pilgrim's Progress*).

104   *last ... saints* i.e. as they await the millennium (see IV.v.26 n.)

105   *Six ... ten* i.e. 1610, the year of the play's action.

111   *Gad in exile* i.e. the exiled brethren (see Genesis 49:19).

117   *Harry Nicholas* Henrick Niclaes, Anabaptist leader of a sect known as 'the family of love', against which Elizabeth I had issued a proclamation in 1580.

121   *Westchester* Chester.

126   *tupped* mated (used of sheep).

127   *But ... lady-tom* except by a knight, to make you a lady.

128   *mammet* puppet.
      touse beat.

129   *mun'* must.

131   *feize* (1) beat, flog; (2) do for.

132   *buckle ... tools* draw your weapon.

134   *change your copy* change your pattern of behaviour.

135   *stoop* swoop (as a kestrel on its prey).

139   *and* if.

144   *Jovy* jovial.

152   *candour* (1) good name; (2) integrity.

154   *canon* rule of behaviour.

159   *decorum* dramatically appropriate.

162–3   *I ... country* I appeal to you as the jury.

164   *quit* acquit.

165   *guests* implying that the audience are as much dupes as Dapper, Drugger, Mammon *et al.* (see 'To the Reader', ll.2–4 n.).

THE PRINCIPAL COMEDIANS

The parts are likely to have been taken as follows: Burbage (Face), Lowin (Mammon), Condell (Surly), Ostler (Lovewit), Heminges (Subtle), Underwood (Dapper), Armin (Drugger), Cooke (Ananias), Tooley (Wholesome), Eccleston (Kastril). Doll was probably played by John Rice, not listed here.

Glossary of alchemical and related terms

ablution   washing out impurites
adrop   (obscure) (1) lead (?); (2) the stone (?)
alembic   a distilling apparatus consisting of a cucurbite (q.v.) and a helm (q.v.)
alkali   caustic soda-ash
aludels   pear-shaped earthenware pots, open at both ends, and used as a series of condensers in the process of sublimation (q.v.)
amalgama   a mixture of metals with mercury
antimonium   antimony
aqua regis   (Lat., 'king's water') a mixture of nitric and hydrochloric acid, used as a solvent for gold.
aqueity, terreity and sulphureity   the sublimation (q.v.) of mercury would remove the first two of these, purifying it of the baser elements of water and earth
argaile   crude cream of tartar
argent-vive   quicksilver
ascension   refining, distillation
athanor   a 'digesting furnace' maintaining constant heat by the continuous feeding of charcoal through a tower
azoch   (1) mercury; (2) (obscure) perhaps also the philosopher's stone

balnei, balneo   (Lat., 'bath') a bath of sand or water used for gradual heating; the second-lowest grade of heat used in alchemy

balneo vaporoso   (Lat.) a vapour bath.

bolt's head   'a globular flask with a long cylindrical neck' (*OED*)

bufo   (Lat.) toad (q.v.)

calce, calx   the residue after calcination (q.v.)

calcination   burning a substance to powder; hence **calcine** (v.)

ceration   see *inceration*

chibrit   sulphur

chrysopoeia   (Gr.) gold-making

chrysosperm   (Gr.) seed of gold

cibation   the seventh stage in the conversion of base metals into gold; feeding in fresh substances to compensate for evaporation

cineris   (Lat., 'ashes') the second grade of heat (see *balnei*)

cinoper   cinnabar, red mercuric sulphide

circulate   as in a pelican (q.v.)

citronize   to achieve the yellow colour indicating 'complete digestion'; between the white and red stages of the process, one step away from success

cohobation   repeated distillation

crosslet   crucible

crow   the blue-black colour indicating progress in the experiment

crow's head   see *crow*

cucurbite   a gourd-shaped retort, the lower part of the alembic (q.v.), holding the substance to be distilled

digestion   dissolving in a slow heat

dragon   mercury

dulcify   (1) wash the soluble salts out of a substance; (2) neutralize acidity

elixir   (1) that which changes base metals into gold, sometimes identified with the philosopher's stone; (2) an essence
with the power to prolong life indefinitely; (3) a sovereign
remedy for all disease; (4) the quintessence (q.v.), soul or
secret principle of a thing

embrion   the earliest stages of the process

equi clibanum   (Lat., 'horse's oven') the heat of horse-dung,
the lowest heat used by alchemists

exalt   to raise a substance to a higher degree, i.e. to purify or
concentrate

faeces   sediment

ferment   an agent that causes fermentation (q.v.)

fermentation   the sixth stage in the conversion of base metals
into gold

fimus equinus   (Lat., 'horse-dung') see *equi clibanum*

filter   a cone of brown paper in a glass funnel

firmament   the sphere beyond the planets, in astronomy the
purest region, hence 'the philosopher's stone'

fixation   transforming a volatile or fluid substance to a stable
or solid state; hence **fixed**

flower   the refined essence of a thing or substance

flower of the sun   the philosopher's stone

furnus acediae   (Lat., 'furnace of sloth') see *piger Henricus*

glorify   to refine or sublime; hence **glorified spirit**

great med'cine   the philosopher's stone

gripe's egg   a pot shaped like a vulture's egg

ground   sediment

heautarit   mercury

heighten   to purify

helm   the long-beaked cap of the alembic (q.v.), carrying
vapour from the cucurbite (q.v.) into the receiver (q.v.)

Hermes' seal, signed with   hermetically sealed by heating
and twisting the glass neck of a vessel

ignis ardens (Lat., 'fierce fire') the hottest fire
imbibition steeping in a liquid
inceration moistening to a waxy consistency
incombustible fixed; see *fixation*

kemia either (1) chemical analysis or (2) a cucurbite (q.v.)

lac virginis (Lat., 'virgin's milk') mercury
lapis mineralis (Lat.) the mineral stone, 'perhaps thought of
  as the *matrix* or mother of minerals' (Mares)
lapis philosophicus (Lat.) the philosopher's stone
lato latten, a mixed metal similar to brass
limbec see *alembic*
liquor of Mars molten iron
loose (as a verb) dissolve
Luna (Lat., 'moon') silver
lunary the fern moonwort; perhaps its liquor was connected
  with the manufacture of silver
lute stop a vessel with clay
lutum sapientis (Lat., 'philosopher's clay') paste for sealing
  vessels

macerate soften by soaking
magnesia (obscure) perhaps one of the 'metals of the alkaline
  earths' (*OED*)
malleation hammering, the *proper passion* (II.v.29) or dis-
  tinguishing physical property of metals
marcasite white iron pyrites
married combined
Mars the planet of iron
materia liquida (Lat.) liquid matter
materials the basic ingredients for the making of the stone
medicine see *elixir*
menstrue a solvent; **loosed ... I' their own menstrue**
  (II.iii.71–2), dissolved in their own distillation
menstruum simplex (Lat.) simple solvent
mercury quicksilver

mercury sublimate   chloride of mercury
moon   silver
mortification   destroying the active qualities of chemical substances, the opposite of vivification (q.v.).

nipped   sealed; see *Hermes' seal*

oil of height   (obscure) perhaps (1) 'oil of nature', the salt that is the essence of all salts, or (2) oil of Luna (q.v.)
oil of Luna   white elixir

panther   spotted colouring
pelican   a vessel with a long curved neck in which vapour condenses and is carried back into the vessel to be resublimed (see *circulate*)
perfect ruby   the philosopher's stone (the ruby colour indicated the final perfection of the process)
philosopher   alchemist
philosopher's stone   see *stone*
philosopher's vinegar   either (1) mercury or (2) metheglins vinegar, used as a solvent
philosopher's wheel   the alchemical cycle or series of processes
philosopher's work   the stone
phlegma   'any watery inodorous tasteless substance obtained by distillation' (*OED*)
piger Henricus   (Lat., 'lazy Henry') a multiple furnace heated by a single fire
projection   the culmination of the alchemical process
propria materia   (Lat.) a specific substance
putrefaction   decomposition, disintegration or separation

qualify   dilute a corrosive liquid
quintessence   the 'fifth essence' of which the heavenly bodies were composed, and latent in all material things; the essential principle of any substance, above the four elements that constituted matter

receivers   see *recipient*
recipient   condensing vessel in the distillation process
rectified   distilled
rectify   purify
red   (1) the colour indicating the successful completion of the alchemical work; (2) pertaining to sulphur
red man   sulphur
register   a damper controlling the draught to a furnace
reverberating   heating in flames reflected downwards from the top of the furnace

St Mary's bath   a water bath (see *balneo*)
sal-tartar   carbonate of potash
salt of mercury   mercuric oxide
sand heat   the heat of a sand bath (see *balneo*)
sapor pontic, sapor styptic   (Lat.) two of the nine 'savours' or tastes in alchemy, these two indicating degrees of sourness
sericon   (obscure) a 'substance supposed to be concerned in the transmutation of inferior metals into gold' (*OED*)
silver potate   liquified silver
Sol   (Lat., 'sun') gold
solution   transformation of a solid or gas to a liquid by using a solvent
solution, giving him   dissolving it
spagyrica   'separating and bringing together' (Paracelsus' description of his essential method)
spirit   material substances for Paracelsus had three primary 'bodies': salt (body), sulphur (soul) and mercury (spirit)
spirit of Sol   (obscure) perhaps the essence or distillant of gold
stone, the philosopher's   a substance with the reputed property of changing metals into gold; often identified with the elixir (q.v.)
sublimation   the conversion of solids into vapour by heat in order to refine them; hence **sublimed**, refined
sulphureity   see *aqueity*
sulphur o' nature   combined with mercury, it made gold

sun gold
suscitability volatility

terra damnata (Lat., 'condemned earth') sediment
terreity see *aqueity*
tincture (1) 'the quintessence [q.v.], spirit, or soul of a thing'
  (*OED*) (see *elixir*); (2) the extraction or infusion of this
  essential principle; hence **tinct** (v.)
toad black colour appearing during the alchemical process
tree of life the philosopher's stone
triple soul the essence of a substance, thrice refined
turris circulatorius (Lat., 'circulation tower') an apparatus
  for the continuous sublimation of materials (see *pelican*)
tutty crude zinc oxide

ultimum supplicium auri (Lat., 'extreme punishment for
  gold') the addition of antimony, which makes gold less
  malleable

vegetals (1) vegetables; (2) all living and growing things
Venus the planet of copper
vitriol sulphuric acid
vivification restoring a substance to its natural, pure state

white pertaining to mercury
white oil, white woman mercury

zernich orpiment, trisulphide of arsenic